Praise for *Are You Living with a Narcissist?*

Laurie Hollman artfully reframes the delicious notion of healthy infantile narcissism that makes babies so irresistible and entertaining, but when exaggerated by troubled adolescents and grown men in malignant or malicious ways, this quite difficult brand of self-preoccupation creates major upheavals and chaos in personal relations. Hollman invites the reader to venture into the lonely world of males striving to complete themselves through an illusion of self-sufficiency and self-importance, in which family members or close others are expected to fill the deeper narcissistic void by becoming a devoted audience or a stunning, libidinal ideal. Hollman brings us stories of family origins of self-love gone astray. Professional or financial success for a narcissistic male covers over deep pain and resentments of lost love, usually occurring within the initial three years of development. Throughout the pages, we view the male narcissist's many attempts at controlling others to ensure entitlements or adulation; with rageful, depressing consequences when frustrated or disappointed. The chapter on self-psychology and [Heinz] Kohut in particular resonates with the notion of how important mirroring was and still is to the narcissistically impaired, and families are likely to benefit from the non-pathological explanation of problems with narcissistic relating, and from carefully reviewing Hollman's evocative examples throughout the book.

Hollman's chapters are well crafted and informative, appealing to a wide audience: Mental health professionals, men, and their family members can benefit from the themes and poignant reflections on the evolution cultural content, together with detailed family systems material. Another audience for this volume are high school health class teachers, who deal with young people every day. Adolescents are striving for direction in learning coping skills in a world of social media saturation; adolescent yearnings will find rich materials for classroom exploration and in-home family conversations.

The book has no happy endings. What is clear in the reading is that Laurie Hollman's experiences and exposures to narcissistic extravagance, in treatment and in observations of families over time and culture, leads to an insightful conclusion: Rearing a stable, resilient, and satisfied child is not a matter of all or none. No one size fits all. Optimal frustration combined with affection, guidance, and give-and-take are most useful tools. Narcissistic supplies are nurturing throughout life. Everyone benefits from self-awareness and awareness of other's needs. Mutuality may not be easily acquired, depending on how narcissistic strivings are processed in family life. Hollman's new book offers a primer that is a guide to learning and thinking seriously about how we raise children, males in particular. While mother's role is emphasized, male and female parents have opportunities to pick up on the *what* and *how* male children require a particular sensitivity to what is expected of them throughout early development.

—Carl Bagnini, LCSW, BCD, psychoanalyst; The Adelphi Derner Postgraduate Programs in Psychoanalysis, and Couple Therapy; faculty, Adelphi Doctoral Clinical Psychology Program

Dr. Hollman provides a fascinating look into narcissistic personality disorder in men from its origins in the first three years of life to its manifestation in adulthood, noting the nuances between healthy self-esteem and pathological narcissism. As she did in her groundbreaking book *Unlocking Parental Intelligence: Finding Meaning in Your Child's Behavior*, Dr. Hollman combines compelling research with compassionate real-life stories that illustrate how women (mothers, daughters, and wives) can make sense of—and better manage—these complex relationships. From how not to raise a narcissist to living with one, Hollman provides a probing perspective on a timely topic that, at times, seems to be a national epidemic.

—Marcelle Soviero, former owner and editor-in-chief, *Brain Child* and *Brain Teen* magazines; author, *An Iridescent Life: Essays on*

Motherhood and Stepmotherhood; editorial advisory board, *Creative Nonfiction Magazine*; founder, Marcelle Ink, coaching and consulting for writers and creatives

Dr. Hollman brings thoughtful and compassionate insight into the formation and perpetuation of the narcissistic personality from multiple perspectives and contexts. By incorporating her Parental Intelligence approach, fresh discoveries from her clinical work, and established models of intervention, Dr. Hollman's book will serve as a useful guide for couples, families, and professionals to identify and more effectively deal with elements of narcissism and create a foundation upon which to build new family legacies of health and recovery.

—Lynn Seskin, PsyD, clinical psychologist; Behavioral Medicine Associates of New York; Behavioral Medicine of Pennsylvania

Are You Living with a Narcissist? How Narcissistic Men Impact Your Happiness, How to Identify Them, and How to Avoid Raising One by Laurie Hollman, PhD, offers timely insights into a range of narcissistic types, from a healthy narcissistic stance through pathological and exploitive narcissism. Dr. Hollman has created a work that has woven her own clinical experience and discussion of case studies, blending potential psychotherapeutic interventions with clinical sensitivity. The integration of current DSM-5 criteria within a psychoanalytic framework blends multiple system approaches and is infinitely readable as well as informative. It is appropriate for both mental health professionals as well as for the general public.

—Marcy E. Mostel, MD, psychiatrist and former medical director of CAPE (1989–2016)

An important book for anyone wanting to understand the concept of narcissism and the impact of narcissistic husbands and fathers on wives and children. Dr. Hollman's knowledge and experience are evident in her discussion of the childhood environment that contributes to the development of narcissistic men and her case studies which are very much on target. She provides family members of narcissists clear advice on recognizing and coping with this situation. Readers will find the book interesting, informative and helpful.

—Karyl Gilbert Cole, MD, Distinguished Life Fellow, American Psychiatric Association; voluntary attending psychiatrist, the Zucker Hillside Hospital

Narcissism is a complex clinical concept that has been overused and misinterpreted as it becomes part of the public conversation. Dr. Hollman has provided a comprehensive explanation that will be a great service to those struggling to understand difficulties with their children, spouses, parents, students, and public figures.

—Kathleen Hushion, LCSW, psychoanalyst

ARE YOU LIVING WITH A

NAR CISS IST?

TO JEFF, FOR HIS LOVING COMPASSION AND EMPATHY AS A HUSBAND AND FATHER.

Published by Familius LLC, www.familius.com
1254 Commerce Way, Sanger, CA 93657

Familius books are available at special discounts for bulk purchases, whether for sales promotions or for family or corporate use. For more information, contact Familius Sales at 559-876-2170 or email orders@familius.com.

Library of Congress Control Number: 2019952423

Print ISBN 9781641702331
Ebook ISBN 9781641702799

Printed in the United States of America

Edited by Kaylee Mason, Angela B. Wade, and Alison Strobel
Cover and book design by Brooke Jorden

10 9 8 7 6 5 4 3 2 1

First Edition

ARE YOU LIVING WITH A

NARCISSIST?

How Narcissistic Men Impact Your Happiness, How to Identify Them, and How to Avoid Raising One

LAURIE HOLLMAN, PHD

OTHER BOOKS BY LAURIE HOLLMAN, PHD

- *Unlocking Parental Intelligence: Finding Meaning in Your Child's Behavior* (Familius, 2015)
- *The Busy Parent's Guide to Managing Anxiety in Children and Teens: The Parental Intelligence Way* (Familius, 2018)
- *The Busy Parent's Guide to Managing Anger in Children and Teens: The Parental Intelligence Way* (Familius, 2018)
- *The Busy Parent's Guide to Managing Exhaustion in Children and Teens: The Parental Intelligence Way* (Familius, 2020)
- *The Busy Parent's Guide to Managing Technology with Children and Teens: The Parental Intelligence Way* (Familius, 2020)

ACKNOWLEDGMENTS

First and foremost, I thank my husband, Jeff, for his tremendous support for the evolution of this book. He read it word for word, editing and discussing the many multifaceted aspects of this complex subject matter, narcissism. To write on such a complicated and sensitive topic requires careful feedback and frequent revision, which Jeff offered willingly and expertly. His talents as a careful reader and writer offered me unending support, along with his love and care for me as his author wife.

I am also grateful to my loving family—including my sons, David and Rich, and their devoted wives, Claire and Shelley—for encouraging my writing as it continues to evolve. Writing is an exciting task that requires a great deal of research and concentration that my adult children appreciate, to my great satisfaction. Even their children, my grandchildren, recognize their grandma as an author and instill confidence in my work, which hopefully sets an example for them to follow as industrious, creative young people.

A great deal of thanks goes to the Familius staff, who stayed involved with the production of this book throughout its development. I very much appreciate that Kaylee Mason has been my meticulous and talented editor. Her avid interest in my writing style, as well as the content, certainly furthered the development of my ideas, bringing this book to fruition. I also thank the managing editor at Familius, Brooke Jorden, for her excellent input and considerable participation in this book's publication. I am further grateful to Carlos Guerrero for his expert design of the book covers and to Kate Farrell for her continuing marketing ideas and efforts. I must also include my gratefulness to the Familius publisher, Christopher Robbins, who works so effectively with his team—including me as the author of this book. His accessibility sets an example for his staff that is very much appreciated.

This intriguing focus on narcissism could not have been elaborated without the long journey of my psychoanalytic career and the many professionals (who are too numerous to name) who have influenced my ideas and interest in this significant subject matter. Thank you for all your contributions to my learning and clinical practice.

Upon reaching his manhood, Narcissus incites the passionate love of many, although his invincible pride refuses access to all. The wood nymph Echo is especially entranced by his charms and approaches him with wild embraces to be scorned and cruelly rejected. She wastes away from sorrow, reduced at last to a mere woodland voice.

At the entreaty of Narcissus's rejected wooers, the goddess Nemesis plans a fitting punishment for the boy: that he, too, will become incapable of obtaining what he loves. Thus, when one day Narcissus drinks from a pond, he knowingly falls in love with his own reflection and repeatedly tries to grasp it. He realizes at the end of considerable lamentation that he has been deceived by his own image, and in complete despair wastes away. . . . Echo takes this all in, and with her vestigial voice reintones Narcissus's . . . cries. When the nymphs try to recover his body, they see it has disappeared and find in its place a white and yellow flower.

—*Baker,* Narcissus and the Lover

Contents

INTRODUCTION

The majority of people with a narcissistic personality disorder are men, and in my thirty years of experience as a psychoanalyst and psychotherapist, I have found that of those men, many are highly ambitious and successful. I have chosen to focus on that subgroup—distinguishing this book from the many, more general, all-encompassing volumes that focus on the broad range of narcissists. In this book, I will explore how men with narcissistic traits create toxic family relationships. The book is geared both to the general population, as well as to mental health professionals.

To understand the damaging aspects of a narcissistic personality disorder, it is necessary to view the entire range of narcissistic behaviors and traits, including healthy narcissism. Narcissism is a developmental line that covers a spectrum from normal to pathological. Self-love is of utmost importance as men develop—until it is overestimated with defensive self-inflation that interferes with healthy relationships. What do parents do that result in this inflated sense of self? How can parents raise children not to become narcissists? How can spouses of narcissistic men live healthy, happy lives? The answers to these questions will be explored and clarified.

As a clinician, I am hoping to enlighten my lay and professional readers from a compassionate and objective perspective. I think it beneficial to recognize signs of narcissism throughout its life cycle, as narcissism may wear many disguises, making healthy intimacy difficult.

In my experience, I have met young, malleable narcissists (in their late teens and early twenties) who fortunately seek treatment on their own because of their tendencies to depression and anxiety, self-loathing, and entitlement. Young men with narcissistic tendencies are more open to exploring their traits than older men with similar traits are. Often, older narcissists have some forty years of experience wearing a false persona of excessive specialness, which is often—at least partially—legitimately earned through successes in their fields of pursuit. Their actual success at work woos others in their presence into admiring them, leading to feelings of betrayal when the duplicitousness is discovered. Parents need to understand the transition in men—from normal to pathological narcissism—early on in their child's development.

The older narcissists I have had in treatment come to me because those they have hurt demand it of them; their spouses have been wounded, and narcissistic men fear losing all they have gained in their familial interpersonal connections. In my experience, older narcissists are more intractable to change, but they are not impervious to wanting to live a more satisfying emotional family life.

I will explore the early roots of pathological narcissism in the first three years of men's lives, when they are young children. This crucial time period presages the way a man relates to women when he is older. For example, a one- or two-year-old who has not sufficiently emotionally separated from his mother—due to varied circumstances within the psyche of the mother and the baby—could grow up to have serious narcissistic problems. Infants become fixated with normal moments in time when they feel omnipotent and grandiose, which is normal to do at an early stage of development. However, if that point of development was marred and those moments had an exaggerated impact on the mother-child pair, there can be significant implications years later. This will be discussed and explained further, followed by several illustrations of the problems of narcissistic men.

To preserve the confidentiality and privacy of my patients, names, vocations, identifying details, and unimportant facts about their lives have been changed, but the dynamics remain the same. The men and their families who were in therapy with me are described as composites, not revealing their actual identities.

CHAPTER ONE

Core Characteristics of the Successful Narcissistic Man

The word *narcissism* comes from a Greek myth about Narcissus, a man who sees his own reflection in a pool of water and falls in love with it. One patient said to me, "I'm talking about ME, ME, ME, not anyone else." This self-love, specifically in narcissistic men, is reflected in their exaggerated sense of their importance and attractiveness—not necessarily physically but socially, academically, professionally, and personally. They don't understand why others don't always view them as importantly or as favorably as they view themselves. This mystifies them and troubles them deeply, because this view is so essential to their self-image.

In my experience with narcissistic men in thirty years as a psychoanalyst and psychotherapist, narcissistic men have several characteristics in common. They are exceedingly successful in their professional lives, which makes them attractive to others, and they have high regard for themselves—and feel that they deserve accolades. The narcissistic men I have studied are generally quite wealthy and have superior purchasing power. Despite this outward success, they come to therapy because they are deeply depressed or because their wives threaten to leave them if they don't. They also have volatile relationships with their children, often envying the positive relationships their wives have with them.

Each man with this disorder doesn't have all of the narcissistic characteristics individually, but as a group, narcissists possess all of the traits below. They have a personal sense of their importance and uniqueness—to an extreme. According to the *Diagnostic and Statistical Manual of Mental Disorders*, 5th Edition, 50 to 70 percent of those who fulfill the criteria for a narcissistic personality disorder are men (671).

Here are sixteen characteristics that narcissists generally hold in common:

1. They talk about themselves almost exclusively.

Those with narcissistic personality disorders (NPD) tend to think and speak of themselves most of the time. They are very conscious of their physical appearance, wealth, talents, or achievements (of which there are often many), and they expect to hold your attention to these attributes as they speak. However, their comments may tend to be exaggerated—or at least overemphasized—and are not necessarily accurate reflections of their whole lives. Even when a narcissist's comments are based on reality, the words and stories are repeated endlessly, forcing those within their close environment to hear their stories over and over again, each time someone new arrives. It's taxing to listen to a narcissist's repeated stories, but he likely genuinely believes that he is delighting everyone in his presence. Narcissists would never suspect that others are simply listening to be polite, because narcissists have little regard for those around them. They rarely, if ever, ask others for their thoughts or feelings.

This is because they are centered on themselves and lack empathy, their Achilles' heel. They are therefore unable to recognize or understand the needs and feelings of others, as they don't see themselves as unempathic. Especially in their professional lives, they seem to have an empathic script, but if you know them personally, they disregard other's feelings and beliefs.

2. They have fantasies of greatness.

The minds of those with NPD tend to be filled with elaborate fantasies of success, power, brilliance, beauty, or the perfect mate. Because of these imaginings, they feel they should have the best of everything, including houses, cars, clothing, or other status-affirming things, like their level of medical care and where they attend school. Sadly, these wishes, or fantasies, are a way for narcissists to fend off inner emptiness and shame and instead feel special and in control, avoiding feelings of defectiveness and insignificance.

Young, budding narcissists are more open to explaining and exploring their lack of an inner core that they hope to fill with others' admiration. In older men this exploration is denied at first, because narcissistic men are rarely rooted in reality. Thus, they experience immense frustration and anger when their visions are not achieved.

Men with NPD often have a grandiose sense of self-importance, leading them to feel superior to others or that they should always be in the company of greatness. They believe that only others who are just as special as they are can truly understand them, and those are the people they want to be surrounded by. To maintain feelings of superiority, they will resort to disparaging others by focusing on others' flaws—whether real or imagined. For narcissists, this is an effective way to hide (and project) their own shortcomings and preserve their self-image. If those they are speaking to or about tend to question the reality of the narcissist's word, *their* beliefs—not the narcissist's—are minimized, or at least questioned, because the narcissist is so convincing.

3. They require constant praise.

Despite how outwardly confident narcissists may portray themselves to be, they are often quite vulnerable and insecure, with fragile self-esteem. To continually prop themselves up, they expect—and thus require—near-constant attention, praise, and admiration. They also may expect to be recognized as superior even without achievements that warrant it. Due to their fragility, when it comes to their sense of self, narcissists are highly reactive to criticism that they don't feel they deserve. Any comments that shine a spotlight on their deepest inse-curities or flaws may be met with a burst of *narcissistic rage*, causing the person to lie or divert the conversation in an entirely different direction.

4. They experience a sense of entitlement.

People with NPD tend to believe that others ought to offer them special favors and fulfill their requests immediately, without question. If such treatment isn't given to them, they may become impatient or angry or give others passive-aggressive silent treatment, because they view others as existing primarily to serve their needs and don't have regard for others' wants and desires. This behavior is akin to the ego-centric toddler who never learned he is not the center of the world and becomes enraged when others don't meet his immediate demands. As children, narcissists were often extremely demanding, threw temper tantrums, and needed insatiable attention.

5. They take advantage of others.

Many people are naturally drawn to narcissists—finding them attrac-tive, charismatic, and exciting—and want to be a part of their lives, which the narcissist expects to be the result. Thus, most often people with NPD do not have any issues getting people to do what they want. They are easily bored and seek constant entertainment, whether their partner wants to participate or not. The partner tends to give in and go where the narcissist wants for entertainment; because otherwise the narcissist passive-aggressively broods and scowls for not getting his way. But in cases where the narcissist's needs are not being met, he will have no problem taking advantage of others—with little to no regard for the feelings or interests of these people. As a result, narcissists often have tumultuous "friendships" and romantic attachments that are either short-lived or long-term but always suspect. If they have long-term relationships, they are easily disloyal to their spouses and friends, lying and cheating with little or no remorse if they are not caught.

6. They are envious of others.

Experiencing envy is another common symptom of NPD. Because of their low self-esteem and need to be superior to others, narcissists see people who have things they don't—such as tangible items, status, or admiration—as threats. They don't understand why they don't have everything they want when they want it, and they seek vengeance toward those who seem to stand in their way of getting satisfactions that they feel are their due. Narcissists may also believe that others are envious of them. And while this is exactly the type of attention the narcissist wants, when he accuses people of such feelings, it often puts an eventual end to the relationship or confuses the other person, who is trusting and innocent of the accused characteristics.

7. They relish being the center of attention.

Since narcissists need constant praise from others to feed their low self-esteem, and because they ironically feel superior to others at the same time, they crave attention and will often seek it out quite effectively. Narcissists dominate conversations. They feel compelled to talk about themselves, and they exaggerate their knowledge and accomplishments.

There are different characteristics of narcissists that stand out, such as the grandiose, thick-skinned narcissist and the vulnerable, thin-skinned type. It's the grandiose narcissist who craves attention and often receives it by being outspoken, arrogant, self-loving, and entitled. The vulnerable type lives in fear of not being admired and accepted by those with the prestige and status that he feels he deserves to be a part of.

8. They lack empathy.

As noted above, narcissists often lack empathy. They are unable to empathize with others or understand that others may have struggles of their own. If they recognize others' struggles, they don't understand why these people don't change according to the narcissist's needs. They seem to have an inability to recognize the needs and feelings of other people. They don't understand why others don't always view themselves from the narcissist's perspective. Sometimes, a person with NPD can seem totally reasonable—until they say something that's provocative and insensitive.

9. They have boundless ambitions.

Having goals or ambitions in life is a good thing, but narcissists make their dreams the center of their world and expect others to want for them what they want for themselves. Because they feel superior to others and want to believe that others find them naturally special, they often set endless ambitions for themselves. Narcissists fantasize about not only *doing* their best but *being* the best, and when they fall short, they are enraged or deeply disappointed to the point of depressive negative thinking about themselves. This then causes them to focus on how they aren't as powerful, beautiful, or wealthy as they think they should be or deserve to be. This sense of entitlement and superiority is why they tend to associate themselves with "high-status" people and obsess over status symbols (from the right shoes to the right cars)—even demeaning anyone they don't perceive to be part of the same exclusive club. This can be quite literal, as they attempt to join and be accepted by prestigious clubs. When they fall short, they are devastated and angry and take a long time getting out of their dilemma.

10. They are incredibly insecure.

This may sound counterintuitive, because when you first meet narcissists, they come across so charming, entitled, and confident. However, people who suffer from narcissism are usually incredibly insecure, which is why they feel the need to put others down. They often speak of people who are liars (disloyal friends or coworkers) when they themselves share the same characteristics that they are unconsciously denying.

Because there are both grandiose and vulnerable types, the former is more outspoken, while the other is more introverted. The insecurity of vulnerable narcissists often seems to stem from the fact that they internally question whether they are truly special and unique; therefore, they are more likely to seek and rely extensively on positive affirmation from others. They regularly strategize about how to get the attention of those they find superior and ruminate excessively about how to be in the "in-crowd." Networking is part of their everyday life, and they are always seeking confirmation of their perceived greatness.

11. They are remarkably charming.

Upon first impression, narcissists come off as charming and confident. However, as the relationship develops, they can become denigrating of others and aggressive if they are no longer perceived that way. They may gossip impulsively, without regard for the eventual consequence of others rejecting them for this behavior. They seek out positions of power and leadership and will "turn on the charm" to manipulate others into giving them what they want. While people are initially drawn to narcissists' confidence and charm, many find them suspect and conning for attention. While confidence is charming—and those who are successful leaders are often more assertive and demanding—when narcissists don't have as many followers as they expect, they are disbelieving and become enraged. They expect that, with all their strategic networking, they should be extremely popular, and they get deeply depressed when this does not occur.

12. They are extremely competitive.

In a narcissist's worldview, there are only winners and losers; narcissists will strive to be part of the former group without realizing how their manipulations may put people off. They must make themselves out to be superior to everybody else. Their incessant need to win contributes to their inability to embrace another person's success. They inadvertently may put themselves in vulnerable situations where they don't feel superior to their opponents. This is the point. Others are opponents, not just people who have similar aims and ambitions. It's all-win or all-lose, leading to depression if the latter prevails.

13. They hold long-lasting grudges.

On the outside, narcissists seem like they are extremely confident and that they don't care what others think, but they are extremely sensitive and care very deeply about maintaining an idealized image of who they think they should be. As a result, they harbor vengeance toward those who insult them, disapprove of them, or don't give them what they want. They end up holding nasty grudges, because they take criticism—or not being given what they asked for—as a personal attack or assault. When they feel slighted or abandoned, they don't get over it. They feel persecuted and unjustly treated and hold on to these feelings for long periods of time (years), desperately demeaning those in their way. They may claim that they want to dialogue with those who made them feel this way, but in the end, they can't hold an actual discussion, because they do not take others' points of view as possibilities. If someone understands their point of view but still does not take action to fulfill their wants, they are offended, feel disrespected, and seek to punish them.

14. They find criticism intolerable.

Most of us have experienced a time or two when we've become frustrated over things not going our way, or we have had a hard time taking criticism from others. It's natural and human. But when it comes to narcissists, their inability to handle fault goes deeper. They have difficulty coping when things don't go their way, and they will be hard-pressed to ever admit fault when they are wrong, which makes it very hard for them to take any kind of criticism, even if it's constructive. They hold the criticizer up as the person who made them a loser, thinking they never deserved it. They cannot bear the insult and need a lot of space on their own to recover and get back into the fray. They may react to criticism with outbursts of disparaging others ruthlessly, yelling, crying, and denigrating others who are close to them and care about them.

15. They are constantly on the go, not to feel boredom.

Narcissists push others to attend concerts, plays, expensive dinners, and prestigious parties, because they can't be idle. To be idle is to feel the inner tension of maybe not being as superior as they believe. Others are put off by this constant pressure to "do," but the narcissist can't relax alone or enjoy their own company, except as a respite from their inner strivings. They may tend to travel extensively and feel they deserve the best accommodations in planes and hotels. Often wealthy, they may obtain these traveling needs by insisting on sitting in business class.

16. They need total control.

The narcissist wants to control others, so they lead instead of follow. They will make all the travel arrangements and schedule all appointments, leading their entourage. They don't care if this bothers others, because they are unaware of their sense of well-deserved leadership at any cost to others' needs. They subjugate others in these endeavors without thinking of others' feelings or any alternative plans to their own. They text and call persistently to make sure their objectives are first and foremost in everyone's minds. They expect others to drop what they are doing to respond to these constant contacts and find it is only *their* schedule that matters. They stay very busy in order to ward off any boredom and a sense of emptiness.

They may do very kind things for others, especially in their professions. However, it is not out of deep caring for others, but to be *perceived* that way. They collect people who adore them excessively in this way. They are always on the lookout for being recognized. Because they see themselves as larger than life, it only makes sense to them that they control others' plans; they are the center and demand and expect others to see them that way. They are the most important person in the family, the CEO and COO wherever they go.

On their birthdays, or other days that highlight their importance as fathers or husbands, they expect large gatherings that applaud them. Then they control these events by being at the center of all their guests. They glower at others who don't both put them in control and meet all their needs—like a child in a toy store with parents of endless wealth. Narcissists assume that they are the star, and they will gladly walk out on any crowd—even if gathered on their behalf—or give the silent treatment if they feel any measure of disappointment. Ironically, guests often go along with this and feel that they should not disappoint this self-acclaimed star; they may even fault and berate themselves mercilessly and urgently if things don't go according to the narcissist's plans to be the center of attention. He, the narcissist, is the captain of the ship; the guests are just the dutiful passengers affirming his greatness. The narcissist manipulates with gifts and conversation starters, only to come back to himself as the center.

The Diagnostic and Statistical Manual of Mental Disorders, 5th Edition, Diagnostic Criteria of the Narcissistic Personality Disorder

"A pervasive pattern of grandiosity (in fantasy or behavior), need for admiration, and lack of empathy, beginning by early adulthood and present in a variety of contexts, as indicated by five (or more) of the following:

1. Has a grandiose sense of self-importance (e.g., exaggerates achievements and talents, expects to be recognized as superior without commensurate achievements).
2. Is preoccupied with fantasies of unlimited success, power, brilliance, beauty, or ideal love.
3. Believes that he or she is special and unique and can only be understood by, or should associate with, other special or high-status people (or institutions).
4. Requires excessive admiration.
5. Has a sense of entitlement (i.e., unreasonable expectations of especially favorable treatment or automatic compliance with his or her expectations).
6. Is interpersonally exploitative (i.e., takes advantage of others to achieve his or her own ends).
7. Lacks empathy: is unwilling to recognize or identify with the feelings and needs of others.
8. Is often envious of others or believes that others are envious of him or her.
9. Shows arrogant, haughty behaviors or attitudes" (669–670).

CHAPTER TWO

The Spectrum: From Healthy to Pathological Narcissism

Healthy narcissism is defined as having a realistic self-esteem without being cut off from an emotional life that can be shared with others. The concept of healthy narcissism developed slowly out of the psychoanalytic tradition and became popular in the late twentieth century. On the following page, you'll find a summary of the major differences between healthy and pathological narcissism for parents to consider as they raise their children:

CHARACTERISTIC	HEALTHY NARCISSISM	PATHOLOGICAL NARCISSISM
Self-esteem	High self-confidence in line with reality, including body image	Self-aggrandizement; belief in omnipotence
Wish for power and admiration	May enjoy power	Pursues power; lacks normal inhibitions and limits
Relationships	Real concern for others and their ideas; does not exploit or devalue others	Socially appropriate responses when convenient; devalues and exploits others without remorse
Values and aspirations	Has values; follows through on plans	Deficient in consistent societal values; readily bored
Formative childhood development	Healthy childhood with support for self-esteem and reasonable limits of behavior toward others	Traumatic childhood lacking sufficient empathy and attunement; wasn't taught consideration for others

Narcissism exists on a developmental spectrum. Heinz Kohut (1971) believed there was a developmental line for narcissism, which contributed a great deal to the understanding of pathological narcissism. According to Kohut's self-psychology model, narcissistic psychopathology is a result of parental lack of empathy during early development. Thus, parents need to carefully consider their empathic relationship with their children. Empathy means sharing with your children your understanding of where they are coming from, getting into their shoes from early on. If this is not done sufficiently, the child does not develop the full capacity to regulate his self-esteem.

What if the parent does not help a child regulate his self-esteem by appropriate and realistic attunement to his development? The future of that child becomes one of a narcissistic adult who, according to Kohut's concepts, vacillates between an irrational overestimation of the self and irrational feelings of inferiority. This child as a man continues to rely on others to regulate his self-esteem and give him a sense of value. In treatment, Kohut recommends helping the patient develop these missing functions by empathizing with the patient. Early on, teaching in this way is the function of the parent, and if it is not communicated, it can leave the child with a deficit of needed realistic admiration and approval.

Kohut believes that under normal circumstances, the developing infant has two important psychological constructs: the grandiose-exhibitionistic self (normally evolving into self-assertive ambitions) and the idealized parental image (normally evolving into internalized values and ideals). Pathology in the first area results in grandiosity, and pathology in the latter results in deficits, where the psychopathology stems from early idealizations.

Thus, the parent who is not sufficiently and accurately empathic with her young child but overemphasizes his attributes—perhaps to satisfy her own longings for a very special prodigy—may lead herself and her child to hold on to a grandiose or elevated image that blooms in narcissistic adulthood. With this elevated view, a child may perceive himself as deserving of special treatment (i.e., entitlement), resulting in acting out behaviors by the child. Such a child may come to expect special treatment from teachers and others in authority. This child will always expect to be regarded as uniquely special and thus have difficulty with peer relations.

Children who do not form normal attachments to others based on trust can grow into adult narcissists. They live in a world of need gratification. These children have unstable attachments with an inability to tolerate frustration, delay, and reality, as their parents have not encouraged them to do so. Because they need to be considered the best, they are extremely vulnerable to frustrations and criticisms. Without the capacity for normal self-acceptance, they suffer endlessly with poor self-esteem regulation, seeking excessive and constant admiration to feel good about themselves. This formative process can presage adult narcissism.

In Kohut's self-psychology model, the dyad between a child and his parent is a continually evolving process. In his theory, a self-object consists of the developing child plus each parent, who gives the child the ability to maintain interior psychological structure and a sense of cohesion and steadiness. "Kohut coined the term self-object to designate the caregiver's support of the infant's self. This term highlights the infant's view of the caregiver as only the supplier of regulating functions that the infant is unable to perform" (Bleiberg 1994, 121). Parents are self-objects, because the infant is unaware that they are not part of his self; the infant is also unaware that they are providing functions the infant will later learn to do on his own, as these functions are incorporated into his psychic (cognitive and emotional) structure. When certain self-object needs are not met empathically, a developmental arrest occurs—and pathologic narcissism can occur. In summary, the self-object is the caregiver's support of the infant's self. This term highlights the infant's need for the caregiver to be the supplier of regulating functions that the infant is unable to perform on his own (Bleiberg 2001).

In Kohut's model, when certain self-object needs are not met empathically, a developmental arrest or fixation occurs, and pathologic narcissism can result. Parents need to be advised to empathize accurately and realistically with their child's development.

For example, the demands of the child with budding features characteristic of a later diagnosis of NPD (narcissistic personality disorder) who grows up to be an adult narcissist are excessive compared to the normal child, whose dependency and demands on those around him are realistic and can be met. The child with such features of NPD is coercive in his demands and feels no gratification nor appreciation when he gets them satisfied. Additionally, he does not recognize any anger felt by the parent. Narcissistic supplies (love and admiration) are never enough to satisfy the demands of the grandiose self of this child. No matter how much is given, the child still feels unlovable and unloved. He envies others who have what he wants, which further impedes his ability to get what he feels he needs without resenting others (Kernberg, Weiner, and Bardenstein 2000).

Parents need to consider Kohut's three reasons for this relative lack of parental empathy to occur: (1) a poor fit between the child and parents; (2) the parents are unable to react to and nurture the child; and/or (3) the child has unusually great self-object needs. Whatever the reason, the earlier and more pervasive the failures, the more severe the developmental arrest and the degree of narcissistic pathology in the adult. This is considered a line of development because over time—through just growing up or through treatment—the child develops a more realistic sense of self. Developmental lines show that children naturally develop as they grow.

By describing a narcissistic individual's pursuit to fulfill unmet self-object needs, Kohut describes a certain aspect of narcissism inherent in all of us. Kohut describes the self as the center of the psychological universe and believes we spend our entire lives trying to build and maintain our self-esteem by using self-objects. An example of a self-object is the tie a mother and child have, where the mother is attuned to the child, soothing and affirming him. The mother and child may feel inseparable. However, in contrast to other theorists, Kohut does not believe this type of narcissism to be pathological and argues for continuity between normal infantile narcissism and pathological narcissism.

Parents need to be mindful that Kohut argues that pathological narcissism occurs only with *early* self-object failures, meaning in the first three years of life. When these failures occur, these children search for the gratification of missing childhood self-object needs in their adult lives. They are also fearful of encountering, or repeating, earlier past failures. Therefore, they may present with an attitude of superiority or arrogance, reflecting the anxiety they feel over encountering further self-object failures. This fear may also manifest itself in relationships. Patients with NPD may have a history of many failed relationships, due to disappointment that the relationship is not giving them the longed-for childhood gratification and their missing self-object needs (Muslin 1985).

Kohut emphasizes that we all desire to be perfect, that all of us think of ourselves in a grandiose manner, and that these desires and thoughts are not initially subject to reality testing in the infant. However, with adequate parenting, these ideas are gradually lessened over time (although never destroyed) through inevitable minor self-object failures or optimal frustrations. Parents need to encourage children to adapt to frustrations. These minor frustrations are necessary for shaping a child's sense of self and are not psychologically traumatic. Kohut points out that it would be erroneous to believe parents can (or should) always meet the self-object needs of a child. As parents themselves, they are human and are not always with the child. Kohut believes these failures are necessary to alter the innate, grandiose delusional ideas with which we are born, because they require the child to learn internal mechanisms to self-soothe and maintain his self-esteem, despite not being perfect.

Once parents support their child's ability to tolerate frustration on their own, the child relies less on self-objects (their parents) for appreciation and praise to regulate self-esteem, because the child can regulate it himself. In the narcissistic adult, self-object needs were not met during childhood by his parents, and so these mechanisms never develop, and he will continually look to others (self-objects) for building self-esteem. Therefore, the narcissistic individual is very sensitive to any criticism or apparent rejection (Muslin 1985).

Using Heinz Kohut's self-psychology model, the goal of therapy is to allow the patient to incorporate the missing self-object functions that he needs into his internal psychic structure. Kohut (1971) calls this process *transmuting internalization*, but put more simply, it is the baby's ability to soothe itself bit by bit, as the mother reduces her efforts to intervene when the baby experiences physical or psychological tension. In this way, psychic structure develops, allowing the baby to soothe itself more and more. Loewald (1960) explains that the child internalizes aspects of the parent, including the parent's image of the child. In other words, in the healthy transition, the baby learns to experience himself as centered by being centered upon. This is the empathic parent's function: to accurately and realistically center on their child, whose self-esteem is developing.

If this transition by the parents was missing or insufficient in the baby's life, the baby may (when he grows up) become a patient in psychotherapy, constructing and building new ways to view the world. To achieve this goal, a therapist does not only try to imagine what feelings a certain situation might evoke in a narcissistic patient, but rather tries to feel what that patient felt in the situation. This empathy has been credited with being one of the vehicles for making lasting changes in therapy—making up for the lack of parental attunement early in life. Without this empathic treatment, the patient—whose self is too weak to tolerate more aggressive interpretation—would not benefit from therapy and may, in fact, suffer more damage. In accordance with this idea of providing continued empathic acceptance, self-psychology asserts that it is not wise to agree with, disagree with, gratify wishes of, or provide advice to the narcissistic patient. To do so would change the therapeutic environment from one of empathy to one of judgment (Ornstein and Kay 1990; Baker and Baker 1987).

In Kohut's theory of self-psychology, he asserts that allowing the process of self-development to unfold gradually is necessary in order to gain insight. When interpretations are called for, it is best to provide interpretations that focus on the patient's need to restore solidity and comfort after being injured by broken or failed self-object ties.

To return to healthy narcissism, Sigmund Freud viewed omnipotence and the belief in the magical power of wishes, words, and thoughts in dealing with the world as evidence of the psychological lives of children, thus suggesting the presence of a primary normal narcissism. Freud viewed primary narcissism as the happy state where a baby feels itself to be the center of creation. Narcissism is also viewed as an attempt at self-preservation. That is, self-love is a driving force for self-preservation. When the baby is not sufficiently gratified due to major frustrations he has encountered, he returns to others for love. This is normal and healthy. The infant takes his own body, as well as that of his mother's loving care, for identification.

Kohut believes there are two lines of development. One arises from normal infantile narcissism, which can lead to higher forms of healthy narcissism. The other line goes from infantile narcissism to love of others. Kohut states that these two lines of development coexist in everyone.

Now we can review the healthy self of the grown child who had the good fortune of being raised in the safe and nurturing environment of caregivers giving unconditional love, affirmation, and attunement. This person with healthy narcissism has internalized pleasure in independent functioning with the assistance of the parents (White 1986). In other words, a parent's emphasis on optimal frustration brings about a sense of separateness and fosters the growth of frustration tolerance, capacity for delay, reality testing, and anticipation of the future—all part of healthy self-love.

Another part of the development of healthy narcissism that is important for parents to understand relates to the normal psychic separation from the mother. For the normally developing child, the perception of separateness from the mother stimulates separation anxiety and the experience of loss. This anxiety stimulates the incorporation with the mother. This representation of the mother elicits the internalized representation of a maternal smile. There is thus the illusion that the mother is present and part of the self, leaving the baby or toddler with a feeling of safety. "If the self were able to verbalize its feelings, it would say 'I love me.' Because, in part, *I equals mother*, it

means, 'Mother smiles at me, loves me, nurtures and protects me' "
(Rothstein 1986). The incorporation of this kind of self-love is healthy
and normal in the growing child:

1. A sense of self that is reliably cohesive, good, and whole with
   the continuity of that self-image.
2. An awareness of what the mother thinks and feels that gives
   him the self-confidence to develop and initiate choices, learn
   from these choices, and be his own agent.
3. An experience of the self as the center of initiative that moves
   him toward his aspirations, visions, and realistic ideals with
   resilience.
4. An experience of a sense of confidence and trust in self and
   in others that includes an awareness of reciprocal respect,
   mutuality, honesty, and caring.
5. An experience of mutual respect between self and others,
   including those who have different perspectives so that he
   can reflect upon his strengths and weaknesses, hold himself
   accountable to work on his relationships, and recognize the
   limitations of others while respecting limits and boundaries
   (Payson 2017, 40–41).

CHAPTER THREE

How Not to Raise a Narcissist

The Impact of the First Three Years of Life on Pathological Narcissism in Adulthood

The development of the mother-child relationship during the first three years of a child's life sheds significant light on how adult men come to suffer from confusions over their sense of self in relation to others—particularly with women—as will be illustrated in the later chapters in this book. We will meet several such men with interpersonal difficulties who needed to become attached to women who adored them. This adoration is commonly described as a narcissistic supply that the mother gives the child during his early years. If she doesn't provide this, the danger of raising a narcissist arises. To that end, we will step back to look at the advances in psycho-analytic theories about a child's development during those early years.

There is a stage of child development called *separation-individuation* during the first three years of life. This is when the child must work out his need to feel close to an admiring mother, while also developing a healthy separation where he can tolerate that he is not omnipotent and grandiose—as he once believed as a toddler. During these years, it is required by the mother to help her son experience moments of inner separation where he realistically endures that she is not *one* with him. Although the mother may have shown delight at his experience of being grandiose and powerful, he must learn to temper and regulate these feelings and to wait and delay gratification because, in the healthy development of the child, he must come to know that they (mother and child) are emotionally and physically sep-arate beings.

Parents often wonder how to set limits on their children and why this is so important. Internal separation between mother and child refers to the development of such limits and the experience of differ-entiation between the infant and the mother. When limits are set early on regarding a child's behavior, the child experiences an inner process of mental separation from the mother. For example, when a mother tells her two-year-old, "Use your words, not your hands—hitting isn't allowed," the child knows his mother has a separate vision of how he should behave. They are separate individuals. This cements the clari-fication the child needs that he can't do whatever he wants; he has a mother who is different from him and who may restrict his actions. If she fails to do so, he will feel too powerful and omnipotent, leading to the potential for the development of pathological narcissism as an adult. Children don't want to feel more powerful than their parents. In fact, it's scary for a young child to feel more powerful than his mother. The child needs her to set limits, so that he knows how to relate to oth-ers in a way that is acceptable. If he is too powerful, he expects that he is entitled to more than a child should have. If, for example, the child isn't stopped from hitting his sibling, he feels more powerful than he should and doesn't know how to limit his impulses to express his frustrations and anger. This is a child who could grow up into a narcissistic adult man who feels that he has power and control over others under unreasonable circumstances. He learns to manipulate and coerce others unrealistically when it serves his ambitions.

Individuation, on the other hand, refers to the development of the infant's ego, his sense of identity, and his cognitive abilities. It refers to a developing concept of the self. Although interrelated, it is possible for either separation or individuation to develop more fully than the other in this stage of development, largely depending on the mother's attitude toward the child.

When this period of development does not proceed normally, the young boy becomes fixated, leaving him mentally stuck at the time when he needed great adoration. He does not proceed to the realization that he is differentiated from his mother and cannot expect her to always affirm his sense of infant-like greatness. When this failure to develop occurs during these early years, a man never successfully overcomes these needs for affirmation and adoration. These needs come to characterize his personality, and if he is indeed endowed with a superior intelligence that is applauded too much by his parents, he may be overindulged inappropriately and develop an overestimated sense of entitlement.

Thus, these first three years contain critical formative events between mother and child. Limit-setting, as well as comforting, soothing moments of mother-child unity (Pine 1994)—while they may be brief—take on a great deal of importance in the little boy's personality development. Moments when he magnifies his expectation for maternal relations can impair his recognition of his early identity, leading him to believe he is a person who is not indeed as exceptional as he may have wished to be viewed.

This developmental phase is crucial for a child's later acceptance (as an adult) of his *realistic* power and control over himself and others. He must learn that he is not as extraordinary as he may wish to believe in his interactions with others. Each time he fails to get the recognition he longs for, he may feel very ashamed and vulnerable. This is his plight, his Achilles' heel, his flawed sense of self that can lead to a significant drop in self-esteem and even depression. These early experiences greatly impact an individual's lifelong lines of development, and I will continue to clarify their importance.

Through observations of children and their mothers, psychoanalyst Margaret Mahler discovered that there is an inborn capacity for the infant and child to get interpersonal and intrapsychic (inner psychological) needs from the mother.

In other words, the child unfolds within the environment of the mother-infant unity, setting the stage for enduring patterns that—as we will come to see—become essential to normal or pathological narcissism. The child works back and forth from infancy with his desires to be both part of the mother and undifferentiated (so to speak), as well as autonomous. This back-and-forth process during separation-individuation has a major impact on his development.

> Recent findings about infants challenge these generally accepted timetables and sequences and are more in accord with the impression of a changed infant, capable of having—in fact, likely to have—an integrated sense of self and of others. These new findings support the view that the infant's first order of business, in creating an interpersonal world, is to form the sense of a core self and core others. The evidence also supports the notion that this task is largely accomplished during the period between two and seven months. Further, it suggests that the capacity to have merger- or fusion-like experiences as described in psychoanalysis is secondary to and dependent upon an already existing sense of self and other. The newly suggested timetable pushes the emergence of the self earlier in time dramatically and reverses the sequencing of developmental tasks. First comes the formation of self and other, and only then is the sense of merger-like experiences possible. (Stern 1985, 70)

What this means in practical child-rearing terms is that we don't want the child to feel merged with his mother and incapable of acting in a way separate from her. "Merger" or "fusion" are terms that imply the mother doesn't see her child as a separate individual, but as more of an extension of herself to meet *her* needs. She doesn't differentiate her needs from those of her child. Then the child does not understand that he is a separate individual with strengths of his own—strengths that his mother affirms, admires, and limits realistically.

Taking this new theoretical perspective (that the baby is more differentiated from the mother from the start) does not change, however, the developing narcissism of the adult man based on his experiences in childhood. In a simplistic way, we can observe the development of unhealthy narcissism in families with two different kinds of mothers. In the first, the mother overindulges the boy, thereby not allowing him to escape his inner world of grandiosity. He feels too powerful and may try to coerce others to meet his demands. In the second, the mother is unavailable or rejecting, which causes the boy to desire the inner grandiosity his mother never helped him escape. In this case, if the child feels too much hostility, then love for his parents is overshadowed by hatred. Such an affective (emotional) state would severely impair his ability to negotiate his future development. In psychoanalytic theory, this refers to the development of the Oedipal crisis, which follows the first three years of separation-individuation. The "Oedipus complex" is a term used by Sigmund Freud in his theory of psychosexual stages of development (1914). It describes a child's feelings of desire for his opposite-sex parent and jealousy and anger toward his same-sex parent. This takes place, roughly, from ages three to six (Blanck and Blanck 1974). If the mother or father is too closely connected with their child—as if they are almost a lover—this complicates the child's ability to decipher his role as a child and not a peer with the opposite-sex parent. Children become confused about their parents as "adults in authority" and expect all of their needs to be met at once.

The matter is even more complex when we consider the relatively unseparated state of the parental representations and self-representations (the view a child holds of himself) in severe pathologies. In those conditions, negative emotions color the self-representation, as well as the maternal or paternal representations, severely impeding the progression of the child and young adult's narcissistic development.

In other words, if a child views his image of his parent negatively, it reflects on the child's view of himself. This can occur if the parent isn't successful in setting limits and if the child feels too empowered and at a loss to contain his aggression. Children want to contain their aggression so that they can fit into the social world of peers and adults. If the parent doesn't help her child control his impulses, there is danger of narcissistic development later on when the child becomes an adult.

Of particular interest is the subphase of separation-individuation called *practicing*. Practicing is marked by the locomotion of the infant—usually first by crawling and then by walking. The advent of these physical abilities has a dramatic psychological component. It includes greater self-awareness, due to the viewing of an even larger environment with the baby's great narcissistic pleasures. The infant now has greater capacity for reality testing—no longer just held in the mother-infant dyad—and he begins to realize that he is a small person in a large world. This is crucial for the child to know his place in the adult world and not feel over-entitled to have all his wishes and needs met at once.

This over-entitlement brings on the crisis called *rapprochement*, where the child reacts to the loss of his omnipotence and his oneness with his parents. The resolution of this crisis has major significance for later development, especially the boy's capacity to deal with conflict and normal narcissism.

Conflict remains in the interaction between mother and child if the child's affective (emotional) charge is too hostile toward one or both parents. Then, love for the parents may become overshadowed by some sense of hatred. These feelings impair the child's ability to negotiate conflict with each parent—from whom the child is not sufficiently differentiated. That is, the child has not developed an autonomous self from which to negotiate his interactions with his parents internally and externally. This becomes a life pattern that reveals itself in the adult man's relationship with women. As we will see in future chapters, the narcissistic man views women as there to serve his inner and outer needs, like that of a doting mother whom he has not sufficiently internally separated from.

Intense negative feelings color the relationships, impeding progressive development, such as the capacity for and quality of reciprocal relationships. The mother who enables her child to separate well and develop autonomy gives him a greater sense of normal competence. The mother who prolongs her attachment to her son impedes this development and may lead him toward unhealthy relationships later in life, specifically with women, as he may want the same kind of narcissistic attachment that he held with his mother early on.

Mahler's separation-individuation theory (Mahler, Pine, and Bergman 1975) provides a developmental timetable. This timetable, although it differs from Stern's (1985) perspective, involves the normal infant's passage from physical birth—a state of mostly total dependency and largely unawareness of the boundaries between self and other—to a state of what is termed "psychological birth," which she places around three years of age. This is when the rapprochement crisis occurs.

The narcissistic men that we will study did not wholly succeed in their psychological birth—where the boundaries between self and other were clearly defined, allowing a mutually satisfying marital relationship to form when they grew up. It's as if the child was not properly given enough autonomy to give up a kind of bossiness, which impeded his progressive development. He did not give up reasonable control over his mother, so he cannot feel safe and secure in a relationship and has clear boundary issues with his parents.

Diana Siskind (1994) presents a case of a three-and-a-half-year-old boy who had not yet resolved his separation-individuation phase of development and established his psychological birth, a stage that coincides with the beginning of the Oedipal phase. In his treatment, Siskind adroitly examines how, with her psychotherapy, the boy learned to express and understand the abstraction of the word *no*, said by his mother and said by himself. The understanding of the word *no* facilitates separation and individuation. The word *no* says, "I am not you, mother. I can disagree with you, and you can disagree with me, because we are separate beings." This enables him to move forward, expressing his narcissistic phallic needs during the Oedipal phase—without which he might have had a prelude to a narcissistic disorder, according to Siskind. His ability to seek the approval of his mother and tolerate his and her normal aggressive feelings set him on a normal path of development at this crucial rapprochement phase. This case reminds us that the derailment of these stages of development can lead to narcissistic personality disorders in men.

The definition of narcissism is the relationship with the self or the investment in the self. This is the antithesis of love for another person. According to Heinz Kohut (1966), "The baby originally experiences the mother and her ministrations . . . in a view of the world in which the I-you differentiation has not yet been established" (244, 245).

Kohut explains that the disturbances of narcissistic balance in an adult, referred to as "narcissistic injuries," are easily recognized by the painful emotions of embarrassment or shame, which are often known as inferiority feelings or hurt pride. When the mother does not establish limits and the child grows up, he finds that others do not view him as his mother did. He feels a sense of inferiority that he can't explain, because his mother was not realistic with his abilities, so he expects to be more powerful than is realistic and reasonable. Others find him offensive.

Then there are narcissistic tensions that occur as this child becomes a grown-up who strives unsuccessfully to live up to his ideal (which has been inflated). The superego, according to Freud, is how a person measures himself and his mother. He emulates the mother and strives to fulfill her demands for greater perfection. If she isn't clear that he is not and cannot be perfect, he is prone to pathological narcissism. If, on the other hand, she helps him tolerate his imperfections, this should be the beginning of the development of a conscience. In other words, if his sense of self is inflated, he may not develop a conscience—the inner feeling or voice viewed as a guide to the rightness or wrongness of one's behavior.

Frustrations are demanded by reality, and the child's capacity to tolerate these frustrations leads to his development of normal narcissism. On the other hand, if—due to the mother-infant relationship—such frustrations are not gradually permitted, the child who grows up to be a man cannot tolerate them. Premature discovery of parental weakness because the parents could not give realistic limits also creates conflict in the child. Then, the child does not find idealized parents whom he can admire and wish to be like, but rather parents incapable of allowing him his gradual discovery of shortcomings. This can lead to traumatic pathological results.

At the beginning of a child's life, the idealized parent is gazed at in awe, admired and looked up to. The child wants to become this same ideal. That is, the narcissistic self wants to be looked at and admired. Later in life, the narcissistic ideal is related to the man's ambitions. The normal narcissistic man reaches for his ambitions. The pathological man is humiliated when he fails to live up to his ideals or ambitions.

Then the adult tends to vacillate between an irrational overestimation of the self and feelings of inferiority that are derived from his infantile grandiose fantasies that do not become optimally restrained. While it is healthy to be motivated by ambitions, it is not healthy to love them unconditionally. Then, there are emotions of disappointment that contain shame. This shame results from infantile grandiose fantasies that are not restrained in the adult's personality. He experiences narcissistic humiliation when the admiration and confirmation of his ambitions are frustrated.

It is necessary for the natural exhibitionism of the child to be lessened through gradual frustrations that are accompanied by loving support. There are three parental attitudes that can form a wide range of disturbances: rejection, overindulgence, and—most powerfully—rapid alternations between both. All three of these attitudes lead to heightened narcissistic-exhibitionistic tension that are expressed abnormally by the child. For example, if a child attempts to engage his mother in his exhibitionism but rejection occurs, there is painful shame and the child no longer feels loveable. This contrasts with normal narcissism, where there is healthy enjoyment of one's achievements by the mother and an adaptive disappointment that is realistic (even though marked by some anger and shame over failures and shortcomings).

Kohut (1966) points out that—handled incorrectly by parents, as stated above—normal narcissism can transform into abnormal narcissism in the following areas: "(i) man's creativity; (ii) his ability to be empathic; (iii) his capacity to contemplate his own impermanence; (iv) his sense of humor; and (v) his wisdom" (256).

Let's consider how these five factors are expressed in a healthy person.

1. Creative people tend to alternate during periods of productivity between phases when they think extremely highly of their work and phases when they are convinced that it has no value. This is an indication that the work relates to a form of narcissistic experience.

2. Empathy is an affective cognitive process of feeling, imagining, thinking, and viscerally sensing one's way into the experience of another person. The capacity for empathy lies at the heart of our ability to understand other people. As such, it is central for all human relationships—especially relationships that include intimacy and concern for others. However, empathy can also be misused. It can be used to manipulate, exploit, coerce, and control others—an abnormal narcissistic feature of the personality, compared to its normal growth of the capacity for empathy in childhood. Empathy is often first seen in the three- and four-year-old's ability to take on the experience of another, due to their previous sense of attunement by their caregivers. Empathic responsiveness on the part of caregivers is thus vital to the development of many aspects of the child's psychological life, including the basic sense of self.

3. The capacity to accept one's own impermanence is affected by one's sense of reality. In the abnormal narcissist, this may become a sense that one is so impressive that he cannot be replaced, whereas the normal person values one's self more realistically. Kohut explains that "just as the child's primary empathy with the mother is the precursor of the adult's ability to be empathic, so his primary identity with her [is] . . . considered as the precursor of an expansion of the self, late in life, when the finiteness of individual existence is acknowledged" (1966, 266).

4. He goes on to point out that

> humor and cosmic narcissism are thus both transforma-
> tions of narcissism which aid man in achieving ultimate
> mastery over the demands of the narcissistic self, (i.e., to
> tolerate the recognition of his finiteness in principle and
> even of his impending end). . . . The profoundest forms of
> humor and cosmic narcissism therefore do not present a
> picture of grandiosity and elation but that of a quiet inner
> triumph with an admixture of undenied melancholy.
> (1966, 266)

5. Kohut goes on to define wisdom in the normal narcissistic
   man late in life:

> Wisdom is achieved largely through man's ability to
> overcome his unmodified narcissism and it rests on his
> acceptance of the limitations of his physical, intellectual,
> and emotional powers. It may be defined as an amalga-
> mation of the higher processes of cognition with the
> psychological attitude which accompanies the renounce-
> ment of these narcissistic demands. Neither the possession
> of ideals, nor the capacity for humor, nor the acceptance
> of transience alone characterizes wisdom. All three have
> to be linked together to form a new psychological con-
> stellation which goes beyond the several emotional and
> cognitive attributes of which it is made up. Wisdom may
> thus be defined as a stable attitude of the personality
> toward life and the world, an attitude which is formed
> through the integration of the cognitive function with
> humor, acceptance of transience, and a firmly cathected
> system of values. (268)

Thus, we have seen the remarkable significance of the first three
years of life on the narcissism of a young boy as he grows up to be
a man. His relationship with his mother during his infantile stages
greatly impacts his capacity to develop into a mature, normally narcissistic adult who can express normal intimacy with a woman.

Some Thoughts on How *Not* to Raise a Narcissist

1. Stress the differentiation of the child from the mother and promote his developing identity as an individual separate person.
2. Set reasonable limits on your child's behavior during his first three years.
3. Praise and admire him appropriately based on specific, earned achievements, not globally saying he is always great and special.
4. Teach your child right from wrong so he develops a reasonable conscience.
5. Understand that all young children experience feelings of power and omnipotence naturally, but be cognizant that these feelings can veer out of control in cases of narcissism.
6. Help your child temper his emotions so he can feel them and express them without being overwhelmed by them.
7. Help your child tolerate frustrations, disappointments, and realistic delays in meeting his needs to help him gain resilience in the face of normal failures.
8. Encourage your child to find pleasure and satisfaction in independent functioning.
9. Help your child recognize other people's viewpoints.
10. Value character traits such as honesty and kindness toward others.
11. Recognize and discourage entitled attitudes and actions.
12. Discuss greed and selfishness, and teach sharing with others.
13. Discourage false blame of others for one's own errors and failures.
14. Avoid insisting on perfection, winning, and undue toughness (Barr et al. 2011).

CHAPTER FOUR

The Evolution of a Young Man with Narcissistic Traits

Carver

Carver came to me in late adolescence and continued treatment into his college years. Before I introduce him to you more fully, let me review some of the personality traits associated with narcissism in young people. Narcissism most often refers to the overall well-being of the self, including feelings of aliveness, initiative, authenticity, coherence, and self-esteem in both normal and pathological forms. The narcissistic personality disorder includes defensive self-inflation; lack of a well-formed self-concept; inordinate dependence upon acclaim by others; poor relationships; vulnerability to feelings of humiliation, shame, and rage; depression; and entitle-ment. There is a relentless pursuit of self-perfection with the impaired capacities for concern, empathy, and love of others. Narcissistic de-fenses include self-aggrandizement or omnipotence, idealization, and devaluation—all used to regulate self-esteem.

In 2014, Jean Twenge, author of *Generation Me*, cited that at least 50 percent of contemporary college students in her study scored prob-lematically high in narcissism (xvi). Narcissism, as discussed earlier, includes a vast array of ideas whose common thread or focus is the relationship with the self. These dysfunctional traits were personified by Carver as he grew up.

First, let's think about a very young child in order to ascertain the troubles Carver experienced in his early life. For example, if a young child is overly gratified with respect to normal validation of his self-centered wishes, developmental fixations can be the result. This was the case for Carver. Whenever he asked for his mother's atten-tion—be it for food, play, or praise for his early accomplishments (such as his excellent young vocabulary and ability to read)—she responded immediately. One of the principal consequences for Carver was that the normal balance between self-love and love of others failed to develop in a healthy manner because of his mother's over-attention. If she did not love him in the ways he wanted, such as holding him or listening to him whenever he spoke, he felt injured and unloved. This was not realistic, but he was prone to feeling unreasonably harmed by the normal consequences of large family life. He had five siblings born in close succession when he was young.

In *Richard III*, Shakespeare tells us of Richard's narcissistic inju-ries and his motivation for compensating for them when he says,

And therefore, since I cannot prove a lover

To entertain these fair well-spoken days,

I am determined to prove a villain

And hate the idle pleasures of these days. (act 1, scene 1, 11)

. . . .

All of us have cause

To wail the dimming of our shining star,

But none can help our harms by wailing them.—

Madam, my mother, I do cry you mercy;

I did not see your Grace. Humbly on my knee

I crave your blessing. (act 2, scene 2, 111)

. . . .

What do I fear? Myself? There's none else by.

Richard loves Richard; that is I [am] I. (act 5, scene 3, 287)

These quotations sum up Carver's young and adolescent life to a tee. He was determined to be a compelling presence in his parents' lives. And, indeed, Carver was compelling—because he could not be resilient. If he wasn't attended to, he spoke up vociferously and was very difficult to manage physically, because he would continue to press his parents, especially his mother, for their affection and attention. He always expected to be devoted to and valued.

Self-interest, social responsibility, and concern for others need to be in balance in the healthy personality. Carver lacked this inner balance between concern for himself and others. This was largely due to the impaired relationship with his mother, which was based on all the infantile bliss and power that he felt resided in his (overly) close initial relationship with her. This relationship, in his view, was not sufficiently sustained throughout his childhood and adolescence. The high expectations for her constant availability—which were unrealistic—resulted in his blatant devaluation of her.

As he grew older, she disappointed him gravely by having more children and dividing her initial unparalleled attention to him among him and his siblings. When each baby was born, she attended to that infant intently, feeding and playing with each child, which meant less time with Carver. He was deeply jealous, more than the average child might be when siblings are born. But then again, he had so many siblings (five in close succession) that he felt regularly excluded each time his mother became pregnant and then gave birth. As he grew, he continued to long for his initial, intense emotional proximity to his mother. This became impossible because of her preoccupations with caring for Carver and his siblings at the same time. This paralleled his idealization and devaluation of himself, because although he was favored, he was no longer the only child. He never fully internally separated from her—or her from him. Since all the bliss and power resided in this idealized and, later, devalued woman, as a child and late adolescent Carver felt empty and powerless when he was emotionally separated from her or when she did not fulfill his desires. He thus continued to maintain a continuous pathological union with her. He felt left out and unusually angry. He was unable to tolerate frustration, delay, and disappointment.

This resulted in chronic unstable relationships with his siblings and his peers. It led him to seek perfectionism in others and in himself, as well as find grave disappointment in himself and others when such perfectionism did not surface. He never experienced the gradual disillusionment with his parental images and his self-ideal, which healthy children experience. Thus, he continued to have a hunger for this longed-for state. Further, although he became a young man of considerable intelligence who performed his tasks with skill and creative ability, he was forever in a constant and desperate search of approval and admiration from his peers and adults. He continued to feel he was entitled to this, regardless of how much actual work he performed.

Let's step back and look at early development in order to ascertain how Carver reacted to the normal vicissitudes of growing up. Consider, for example, how during the normal toddler stage of development, narcissism is at its peak. How the parents handle the child's natural grandiosity affects the youngster's capacity for self-regulation and relations with others. A parenting pattern in which the grandiosity of the toddler is limited and constrained in the context of an empathic and gentle approach that helps bring the child back to earth, results in limits set in a reasonable fashion. Then the child is not bound by self-aggrandizement and grandiosity, occurring in the absence of reasonable limits.

Conversely, a child develops an inhibited form of narcissism stemming from too harsh a suppression of the toddler's grandiosity. Carver's mixed responses from his two parents put him in a vulnerable position, and his self-regulation was marred significantly. His mother always tried to put Carver's needs first, ahead of his siblings. This angered her husband, who felt Carver should know his place as an older child and not be so focused on by his wife. For example, if Carver was complaining he was hungry, she would get him a plate of food while she let a baby cry. Carver's father yelled at his wife to stop coddling Carver and take care of the younger ones first; he would banish young Carver from the room and let his wife attend to the other siblings. Carver felt rejected by his father at those times. The father's rage overpowered the mother's compassion. Consequently, Carver could not develop an inner compass that balanced self-interest with love for either his mother, father, or siblings. He would scream at his father for his perception of his mother neglecting his wishes, and his father would yell at him to quiet down. Carver would storm out of the room, feeling enraged at both mother and father.

Because his parents were not capable of helping Carver contain his aggression in the first four to five years of his life, Carver developed a defensive strategy: a rapid rage directed at others. He would first stomp his feet, then lie on the floor flailing his arms and legs, screaming at the top of his lungs. This rage functioned to ward off feelings of helplessness and to maintain desire and involvement with his parents, who reacted differently. His mother would go to him and hold him when he was enraged, while his father would yell at the mother for doing this. Carver devalued his parents but did not relinquish his longing to obtain narcissistic "supplies" from them. He was not a child who would give up and back down. The conflicting values of his parents—the mother coddling, the father holding Carver's arms too tightly in anger— exacerbated Carver's incapacity to develop a secure sense of self.

His mother was unable to set reasonable limits, indulging his temper tantrums, while his father also did not set reasonable limits, conversely reacting too harshly to the normal grandiosity of Carver's age. In other words, it is typical for a two- or three-year-old to want to be the center of attention, especially a child as bright as Carver who could read at an early age. But because there were other small children, Carver's father didn't give him that attention; instead, he dismissed Carver's wishes for praise and approval. His mother's wish for total attunement and availability backfired, contributing to the indulged grandiosity of special children, of which Carver was one. His father's belief in strong punitive disciplinary measures, including creating fear in a child, could not combat his mother's indulgence, a totally confusing situation for Carver. Often, when Carver went to read aloud to his mother, his father would not allow it because of his own preoccupation with power over his son. He would tell Carver to go read by himself and to stop bothering his busy mother. Even as he grew older and became an elementary school child, his father did not give him the praise he deserved for his accomplishments. Instead, for example, he demeaned him because he wasn't athletic, was significantly shorter than most boys his age, and rarely played well in team sports.

The evolution of Carver's aggressive behavior developed out of his attempt to get his mother and, later, his father to accept and understand the meaning of his aggression. In the presence of his parents' failure to understand his anger, Carver felt more and more out of control. His behavior was a way to create a sense of greater control by turning the passive experience of being immersed in his fury into the more active experience of directing his rage at others and getting relatively predictable reactions. By making others feel helpless and out of control, Carver could disavow such feelings in himself and feel more in control. As noted, he cried, had tantrums, and was not easily soothed as an infant and youngster—forcing the environment to attend to him. This continued throughout his adolescence and early adulthood.

Carver's intense and prolonged longing for his mother seemed to have taken the form of an intensification of his aggressive relationship with her as he grew older. His anger was met by her increasing self-doubt in her capacity to mother him. Carver's sense of helplessness was defensively altered through different relationships with each parent. He was the powerful one in the relationship with his mother. He was the power*less* one in the relationship with his father. Narcissistic wishes to be loving were replaced by wishes to be bad. Carver's intense longings for his mother and, later, his father were replaced by angry relationships with each of them.

If the child willingly gives up narcissistic pleasures, such as grandiosity and omnipotence, based on the love of the mother, development proceeds optimally. In contrast, if parental threats are primary in forcing the child's renunciation of such pleasures, the child's reaction can be sadism. The latter condition—due to the dictates of his father—seemed to prevail for Carver at a young age. This foretold his future development, which was apparent as an adolescent where he confused his ambitions and actions. He oscillated between grandiosity and self-deprecation and autonomous functioning. He often felt that he should dictate receiving anything he desired, resulting in a deep interdependence on his parents. This led, as we shall see, to the complex interplay among Carver's grandiosity, entitlement, potential genius, and social and personal values, which often led to rejection from his peers. He failed to understand this rejection and complained of it unendingly.

After knowing him for several months, I decided Carver was not a full-fledged narcissist but belonged somewhere on the spectrum. He was seemingly grateful that I was his therapist and usually came on time and very willingly to each session. He appreciated all that I could help him understand but did not idealize me to the point of agreeing with everything I said, which was healthy. Although he didn't give himself enough credit for his high level of achievements, his deep wish to be accepted into a prestigious university had thankfully been granted. He had expected this acceptance to be the end of all his self-doubts, but it wasn't. Realistically, he still worried about getting along—especially socially in this new environment, where actual royalty from around the world were in attendance. His aim was to become part of their international network, achieve high grades, and graduate as a successful potential candidate for political office. His highest ideal, however, was to be first a delegate to the United Nations and then, once experienced, appointed secretary-general. He was very aware that the

secretary-general is appointed by the General Assembly on the recommendation of the Security Council and that the secretary-general's
selection is therefore subject to the veto of any of the five permanent
members of the Security Council. These aspirations weren't entirely
unrealistic, as he had a very high intelligence, excelled in many lan-
guages, and came from a wealthy family. In their high hopes for him,
his parents had made sure Carver had traveled extensively.

Despite his travels and capacity to live well on his own in foreign
countries, Carver was exceedingly emotionally dependent on his parents. He continued to be particularly dependent on his mother, whom
he denigrated for not giving in immediately to all his demands. At
the same time, he vilified his father, whom he felt fearful of and dis-
trusted. He perceived his father as more brilliant than himself, large
and threatening and often cold. As explained, his father was physically aggressive toward him when he was young. As Carver grew older
and his father sought psychological guidance, Carver's father became
more benevolent and concerned about his pathological son.

Let's step back once again to fully comprehend Carver's emotional development. Remember, Carver learned to read and had a vast
vocabulary at a very young age. His parents had him tested and found
that he had a superior IQ. From that time forward, he was indulged
and favored by his mother—even as five other children were born. He
deeply resented the birth of each of his siblings, because it took his
mother away from him. She did indeed favor him, because she and his
father saw him as a child prodigy who would make them stand out as
having an unusual son. Carver had to respond too early to his parents'
needs and expectations and lost touch with his own awareness and
sense of self. Carver's parents' unrelenting focus on his special abilities
revealed how they unconsciously used his giftedness to meet their own
narcissistic needs.

Carver was burdened without the needed opportunity to simply
be himself and develop other important aspects of his personality.
Regardless of his abilities, his parents' over-attention resulted in a
powerful wounding of his sense of self: he believed he was only worthy because of his special intelligence. In addition, he was denied

empathic but firm limits to guide him. He lost ground in his ability to self-regulate his impulses and feelings, develop empathy for others, and develop accurate self and other observation skills. This resulted in an overemphasis by both himself and his parents on his competitive edge due to his achievements. Early on, Carver's father criticized his wife for her empathy, as he felt fear was the weapon to intimidate and control their unregulated, gifted child.

Carver was indeed awkward among his peers. He felt a sense of not knowing how to relate to others when very young. Then, having so many siblings, he did not want or learn to share and thus had social difficulties in preschool. From that early age, as mentioned above, his focus was on himself—beyond the normal self-centeredness of a small child. As a preschooler, he vengefully messed up other youngster's toys without remorse.

Once in puberty, Carver's pediatrician confirmed that he was not growing according to a normal developmental physical schedule. His parents had brought in eleven-year-old Carver because he was substantially shorter than his classmates and his growth seemed to have slowed in recent years. The doctor concluded Carver had a growth deficiency and recommended the gradual administration of a growth hormone over several years so that Carver would reach normal height. This opinion was shared by a pediatric endocrinologist. Carver's father, a physician himself, wanted the growth hormone protocol because he wanted Carver to be athletic. The mother passively followed along with the father's wishes to comply with the two doctors' recommendation. Of course, to Carver this meant that he was physically inadequate, affirming his worst fears about his appearance. Although he grew into a handsome, tall adolescent, inside Carver sustained the body image of a damaged short boy who was deficient in his appearance and not up to par with other males in his age group.

As an adolescent, Carver berated and competed with his two closest siblings for any attention from their mother. They were physically attractive boys, though not exceedingly intelligent like Carver. He insulted them, blamed them for not meeting his demands, and generally traumatized them with his constant vengeful denigration. These two children indeed suffered greatly from his verbal abuse. He viewed the other, younger siblings as too young to be consequential, but he still felt that his mother and these little girls were too attached to each other.

Let's turn to Carver's mother for a moment to deepen our understanding of his family situation. She was an erratic, impulsive, often frantic but seemingly empathic woman who did not know how to control her children and expect their respect. She was overwhelmed— from her first birth to her last. She was demeaned by her husband for not setting limits and indulging the children. She tried desperately to be a good mother who met her children's needs, but needs turned into demands that overcame her. She experienced vengeful feelings toward those who hurt her children in any way and was prone to be inappropriately overprotective, acting rancorous and antisocial as a result. (For example, when Carver was teased for being little around ages nine and ten, she went to the school and met with the principal, taking out her fury on other parents inappropriately, rather than helping Carver cope with the bullying to secure his self-esteem.)

Carver's mother came from a family where she had antagonistic siblings and parents who were unstable. However, as a young adult she was a successful accountant until she met her husband, a doctor who preferred she remain home to care for their many children: her oldest son, Carver; two sons next in line; and three younger daughters. She did not protest this wish, because she also wanted to be an excellent homemaker. She both admired and criticized her husband; he was a superior provider and well-accomplished in his field of work, but as a father and mate, he was unempathic and hypercritical. Carver's father was a forceful, powerful, highly competitive, angry presence in relation to his eldest son.

Carver's mother never hesitated to tell adolescent Carver that she feared she was not a good mother. She looked to him to be a consoling parent figure for her, which he was not, just as her actual mother was not. She expressed her need for him to say he loved her. He had trouble being outwardly compassionate with her at such moments, yet he seemed moved by her needs. Still, he often denigrated her for her search for pity from him. Her self-preoccupations with being a good mother parentified him to no avail. (A parentified child is one whose role is reversed with his mother or father in that he is sought to parent the parent.) This did not help Carver feel better. In fact, as an adolescent his anger was expressed vociferously, and he cursed at both his parents vigorously. Carver often treated them as if they did not exist as people with needs and feelings.

His aggression was used to defend against his feelings of vulnerability and helplessness. It was his automatic and primary defense against narcissistic injuries and humiliation. His need to get involvement from his parents reflected the intensity of this anger. Over time, the aggression was used in his pursuit of grandiose fantasies of omnipotence. The rage and devaluation of his parents and siblings turned passivity into activity; he subconsciously hoped to defend against his longings for intimacy that threatened to reactivate feelings of helplessness and despair. Yet he never went too far over the edge, because he didn't want to push any family member so far that he couldn't reestablish a sense of a loving connection.

Carver often cried bitterly when he felt his mother didn't understand him. He reported sobbing in late adolescence and early adulthood when his needs were not met. However, his mother only felt manipulated by these crying spells, which is perhaps why he felt emptiness in her presence, rather than the soothing that he sought. This crying was not cathartic for him. It did not release his pain. He knew his mother was suspect of its meaningfulness, but he protested to me that it was authentic, and he was severely pained by her dismissal. However, he noted that one younger sibling would cry on their mother's shoulder while winking at Carver, suggesting that he understood how crying could be a means of exploiting his mother. Conversely, he felt manipulated by his mother when she cried to him and sought his unrequited consolation.

Let's consider what some experts have said about crying:

Crying may be considered as a primitive type of verbalization. Attributing meaning to the different experiences of crying requires the active involvement of an other. Crying is a demand for action from the other. It is a direct and sometimes complex communication between the self and the other. (Alexander 2003, 28)

This was the case for both Carver and his mother, which was never satisfied by either for the other.

Martin (1964) notes that inexperienced or anxious mothers tend to interpret crying as a need for a good feed. He suggests, however, that in many instances the crying infant may be making an attempt to restore psychic equilibrium. Martin goes on to describe how the restoration of psychic equilibrium is established through physical and psychological contact with the mother and the relationship with the self. The experience being that of a metaphorical "good feed." A "good feed" in the clinical setting can be viewed as synonymous with the need for a connection, with the self as well as the "other." (Alexander 2003, 28)

This description seems apt for Carver and his mother—both when he was an infant and a late adolescent. When he cried softly with me, however, I did feel compassion, not manipulation, which I believe he knew. I felt he experienced compassion from me and recognized that my reactions were different than his crying mother's, which contributed to the growth of his more cohesive self and psychic equilibrium during our therapy. This was a new experience for Carver, who would "freeze" his parents "out" when they were unresponsive to his sobbing by not taking their calls and texts for days while he was at the university. This was his attempt to scare them and let them feel some of what he felt; it was a projection of the lifelessness and unresponsiveness he experienced from them as their child. The impotence both parents evoked in Carver by not responding to his crying resulted in this rageful retaliation of "freezing" them "out." In one instance, he hoped they would come for parents' weekend while he would have flown to another state, leaving them pining for him in his fantasy. If he could not find gratification through their love, he would find it through the exercise of his aggression. Furious fantasies were his attempts to compensate for the fearfulness and desperation of feeling unloved.

Carver's early sessions were filled with blaming his parents for not meeting *all* his needs. He confused his aspirations with realistic ideals and an accurate assessment of his self-worth. He was not demanding of me, however, but put me in a more savior category, because he felt so understood by me. My empathy for his self-doubts was the key to our relationship. Feeling understood by an adult was new to him and I believe kept him wanting to come to treatment. I believe he also thought I could change his parents in some way so that they would like him more and give in to his desires.

Unlike other narcissistic patients, he did not idealize me or put me on a pedestal but depended on me to listen attentively to his every word and to be compassionate about his quarrels and disagreements with his parents and siblings. Unlike full-blown narcissists, he could briefly feel empathy for his siblings after he denigrated them, feeling some remorse after identifying with his victimization of them. He was manipulative at the same time, openly describing his motivations to get what he wanted at almost any cost and his inability to enter healthy relationships with his peers.

I believed this mixture of self-absorbed attributes with his self-observed vulnerability, which he could be outspoken about, made him malleable to change (with a significant period of treatment). Thus, these admixtures of traits gave him a possible positive prognosis over the long haul. I understood his abuse of his siblings as envy of their attention by his mother, as well as his attempt to feel some sense of superiority, power, and control in the family. With the third- and fourth-in-line siblings, he would try and make it seem like *they* were always the problem, not Carver.

Significant was his sophisticated belief that he did not have a core sense of self; he was what others wanted him to be. He felt molded by his parents as the high-achieving son but felt unable to meet his father's demands for athleticism as well. Taking the growth hormone helped him look like a potential athlete, as he grew to his full six-foot height, but competitive sports did not come to him naturally—to his father's great chagrin and criticism. As a child and adolescent, he spent most of his time alone, reading and playing with his favorite inventive toys. He created small environments in his home to find peace and solace, such as an overgrown tree in his backyard where he could be found eating snack foods and reading with a sense of harmony.

Overindulgence by his mother, coupled with aggression from his father, exacerbated Carver's temperamental vulnerabilities. His parents certainly did not help modulate them. In addition, his lack of adequate interaction with them kept him from developing the social skills needed to get along easily with others. His parents were unable to tone down his temperamental disposition and prepare him for the larger social arena or to take sufficient interest and pleasure in his abilities in a way that helped him develop a proud sense of competence and belonging in the world. This left him feeling like a lonely outsider at home and at school, which precipitated painful feelings of hurt and anger.

Let's take a moment to consider Carver's father. He possessed narcissistic traits as well. Raised by a very well-to-do large family, he was the favored son. He worked in the same medical practice as his father, unlike the other sons and daughters, who went off on their own (some successfully, and others in debt and addiction). He developed many male friendships due to his athletic prowess growing up and was capable of casual friendships with other couples as a married man. He and his wife were of the country-club set but less needy of being in the highest or most prestigious social groups. This was unlike Carver, who resented them for that.

I saw my initial therapeutic role as mirroring Carver's needs so that he felt understood and cared for. This was new for him, and he seemed to genuinely appreciate my efforts. He knew he was too verbally aggressive with his siblings and mother, but he had mixed feelings about them because he felt they deserved his aggressive complaints. He believed his mother should entitle him to her every waking moment, and he envied and felt vengeful toward his siblings for taking his mother's time—especially the two older boys, who were born after him and grew tall without any medical intervention. He fully let her know his fury at her by brazenly cursing at her, an act which over-whelmed her. Some of the narcissistic rage he felt toward his mother he aimed toward his female siblings. My interpretation of this was that he was attempting to decrease the volume of rage at his mother so that she would not totally reject him.

Regarding contemporaries, he only had scorn for his siblings. With peers, he stayed solitary for the most part. When he was with them, he tried to please them; however, he never felt consistently liked or included. Feeling desperately alone in sadness strengthened his nar-cissism, as he retreated into grandiose fantasies of being uniquely special. His moods dramatically fluctuated between grandiosity and insecurity. When he was the center of attention, he would feel very high, and conversely, when he felt ignored, he would feel depressed. His mother's subtle denigration of his father and her offering the illu-sion that Carver was the preferred child was a form of seduction that encouraged his grandiosity and sense of entitlement. This contributed to his difficulty identifying with his powerful authoritarian father and blurred generational boundaries.

Even though Carver consciously believed that his mother pre-ferred him to his siblings, his sense of self (built on this fantasy) was very fragile. His insecurities, feelings of unattractiveness, and need for constant admiration suggested that he was never sure he was truly admired; he wasn't appreciated for himself, despite his mother's atten-tion. His experience of self was that he was not his own being but what his mother needed to perceive him as (i.e., her brilliant, albeit uncon-trollable, son). This could have led to the paradoxical, joint feelings of omnipotence and helplessness.

Additionally, the intrusion of her image of him created an unreal feeling of being special and must have affected his values and sense of self. Further, the father's identification with or projection of his own specialness onto his son must have increased Carver's grandiosity. As both parents overvalued his achievements, he worried that he wasn't loved sufficiently for himself and couldn't control his environment.

These intrusions of the parental needs interfered with the gradual relinquishing of his natural omnipotence. The parents did not offer age-appropriate frustrations and gratifications but instead imposed aspects of their own selves onto Carver, hoping for fulfillment of their own unconscious needs. This did not permit Carver the gradual development of self-feelings, which would ultimately lead to the establishment of a more autonomous self. The striking unevenness in his self-feelings, both omnipotent and helpless, expressed what is characteristic of a narcissistic disturbance.

Unlike full-blown narcissists, however, Carver could still feel temporary empathy toward others while remaining manipulative and unable to enter healthy relationships. To both his parents and me, it was unclear when he felt genuine remorse. Often, it felt faked. He openly told me he lied to his parents, so there was no reason I shouldn't be wary of his lying to me.

Initially, his investment in our therapeutic relationship was reassuring to me. He rarely showed indifference to me if he missed a session and knew that I had waited for him. For example, he apologized profusely for sleeping through a session. He seemed sincere in his wish to not hurt me or cause me any inconvenience, but I couldn't tell if this was a manipulation to stay in my favor. It was unclear if I could be perceived as a separate individual or only as an extension of his own wishes and needs. Only as I consistently accepted his periodic aggressive absences (he denied any aggression toward me) could he tolerate the idea that I was a separate and autonomous human being outside his narcissistic orbit. I needed to frame my comments in a way that both acknowledged his need to do what he wanted while disregarding others and suggested that he might also care about me and how I feel. Each time he missed a session (especially after my vacations), we discussed my separateness and outside life. Helping him realize that this was okay, I created a place where his worth was acknowledged and his ability to help direct the flow of treatment was intact. I was trying to let him know that external behavior can sometimes communicate what thoughts and feelings do not quite capture. I was both trying to show him that I respected his wishes, which sometimes came across as requests for me to control his parents' decisions about him, while also offering him the opportunity to explore his underlying feelings. In this way, I wanted to show him I was not a version of his parents, but a new and uniquely therapeutic person for him to rely upon—whom he could not control.

Carver didn't date very much. Like many young adolescents, he went out in social groups that were used to affirm and preserve his wished-for grandiose image. His late adolescence was barely different from his toddler years. From his peers, he wanted excessive attention and was aggressive toward others who did not meet his demands at once. As a result, he found himself disliked and living a solitary existence. He sought connections inappropriately with his peers by gossiping about others, hoping for some control and power over them and inadvertently triangulating others into seeking revenge on him for speaking negatively of them. He had the misapprehension that if he confided in one person whom another demeaned, he would gain their favor and friendship. This backfired more than once when the confidante learned he had betrayed them. Instead of becoming part of the peer network he hoped to obtain by gossiping, he was disliked by all involved and frequently excluded.

Carver was pathologically envious of others who had fame and fortune. He mistrusted athletic boys who gained an audience that he couldn't attain. He also wished to be a part of peers whose families were even more wealthy than his own and felt disparaged because he couldn't reach their spending power. He continually negotiated with his parents about how much he could spend. However, he spoke more of regret than blame toward his parents for their lack of even more excessive wealth and prominence.

With his limited dating, Carver became exhilarated when someone that he respected liked him. His longest relationship lasted about four months in college, and his partner found him less important than her other interests. This was a devastating blow to Carver, who couldn't fathom what he had done wrong. Even though his girlfriend's rejection was done respectfully, he saw himself as a loser. Because of his fragile self-esteem, Carver only saw himself as a winner or loser—nothing in between. Losing this relationship was tantamount to feeling destroyed and was an occasion for attacks of rage. (Noteworthy is that this winner/loser split was gradually modified during his course of treatment, as we shall see.)

When someone sought his companionship, Carver doubted their veracity, projecting his own false genuineness onto them. This left him always self-doubting, obsessively worried, and prone to panic attacks, due to his potential self-recriminations for believing in someone's authenticity as a potential friend or partner when it was just a casual acquaintance. He looked to this potential person as a filler of his need for narcissistic supplies, only to feel emptied when they didn't fulfill his hoped-for promise of connection. Unlike the true narcissist who on the surface feels his grandiosity is deserved, Carver felt he was pathologically connected with others, and at first he didn't know how to solve this conundrum that made him feel so powerless, hypervigilant, and in need of therapy.

Part of Carver's plight was his relationship with his father, who, although he genuinely loved his son, had little tolerance for Carver's sense of entitlement. He often threatened to throw him out of the house. They were idle threats, but Carver did not know that. Once, he actually physically attacked his son by throwing him on the couch and then walking out of the room.

It took the boy a long time to learn when his father was serious and when he was bluffing, but he did eventually learn the tactic of idle threats: he would threaten his mother with suicidal gestures that he never intended to carry out. In this way, he succeeded in controlling his frightened mother, who would rush to his side. He felt entitled to these aggressive outbursts; he viewed them as deserved vengeance toward her for not always being available to him in the moment he wanted.

Carver's father used the narcissistic trait of stonewalling, or using the silent treatment, toward his wife and son. He wouldn't talk to either of them for days after an argument. This left Carver feeling deeply injured and excluded from his father's life. His father's pathology prevented him from understanding what his actions did to his son. When Carver wished to communicate, his father only discredited his son's wishes, often saying that if there was a disagreement, then there could be no dialogue. Carver's feelings of helplessness were further increased by his father's intermittent praise of his brilliance. The only times they carried on conversations were in the realm of politics, which lacked the intimacy Carver craved from his father, although underlying their discussions was their common interest in power and control. In many such conversations, his father would first praise his son's thinking, then discredit his points of view.

The trauma during his crucial early development damaged the growth of his subsequent personality, leading to a wounded self who craved the adulation of which he was deprived by his peers, his siblings, and his father. His main narcissistic defenses were a wish for admiration and control over his environment. Once in college, he sought a continuous stream of admiration to shore up his grandiose self to cope with his underlying low self-esteem. He ruminated excessively on being part of an international society that was a fraternity, something he deemed most important in the university; he saw membership in this organization as a future network for his ambitions. Falling short of attaining this acceptance, he fell into a depression that was short-lived, due to his therapy. As a result of treatment, he resiliently sought other connections and sources of admiration rather quickly. This marked significant progress. Although he felt betrayed, he was resourceful enough to seek others to feel a part of (rather than just seeing himself as a helpless loser). This was an important sign. He also began to wonder if he expected too much and was selfish—other signs of progress.

Arabi (2017) points out that "emotional pain keeps us stuck and exhausted, unable to escape the ever-firing stress hormone system that generates signals long after the threat is over" (159). For Carver, this was true of his relationship with his father. His stress response to his father was mirrored in Carver's aggressive relationship with two siblings, who wished to communicate with Carver but to no avail. Thus, generational cycles of learned helplessness and sadistic communication prevailed. In this scenario, I viewed Carver as both a verbal abuser (toward his siblings and mother) and a victim. These circumstances resulted in persistent social anxiety when seeking relationships at the university.

The core of Carver's internal conflict remained the loss of the bliss-ful symbiosis with his mother. This was extremely painful and was the basis for his pursuit of narcissistic perfection—in one form or another. His illusion of perfection was purchased at a painful price, the loss of reality, leading to an internal sense of shame and humiliation, which became a central part of his emerging identity. In contrast to guilt, shame is an emotional response to a cognitive sense of failure to attain ideals and fantasized perfection. Shame was experienced whenever his shortcomings were exposed to his peers. Carver confided in me that he experienced a loss of self-confidence every time he looked at his reflection in the mirror. His lack of real stature had a deep effect on his overly grandiose, internal sense of self. To restore and repair his wounded self-esteem became the central task of his therapy. Originally, he came to therapy with one way of doing this, projecting his shameful self-concept onto his mother and siblings.

Recall that there are two paradoxical aspects to narcissism: grandi-osity and inferiority. To better understand the latter as manifested by Carver, it is worthwhile to revisit Arabi (2017):

> There is an underestimation of the effects of verbal aggression and psychological attacks against an individual which makes up a large component of narcissistic abuse. . . . What people fail to understand is the same brain chemistry activated when we experience physical pain can be activated when we suffer emotional pain. Verbal aggression and social rejection of any kind can hurt, much like physical abuse. . . . According to research . . . the same circuitry associated with physical pain can be activated through emotional pain such as that of social exclusion. (159, 160)

Dr. Martin Teicher (2006) pointed out the growing evidence that verbal abuse in childhood can change the way a brain is wired, increas-ing the risk for anxiety and suicidal ideation in adulthood. There has been corresponding research that confirms that parental verbal aggression can in fact lead to changes in the brain (Choi et al. 2009; Teicher 2006).

This would account for the emotional dysregulation Carver displayed as both a child and a late adolescent: his feelings of not being worthy of inclusion by peers. Potentially, his "brain [had] literally been impaired by the stress of the trauma and the connection between the 'rational' aspects of [his] brain and the emotive aspects" that were impaired (Arabi 2017, 161). This led to a heightened inner critic, which indulged a significant degree of excessive negative self-talk that permeated his everyday thoughts and emotions.

The story of Carver is about a boy raised to be special by parents who early on failed to help him develop a healthy inner mind. His need to aggrandize himself, despite his simultaneous sense of inferiority led him to idealize others whom he deemed worthy of his adoration.

Ideal-hungry, he strove to fit in with leaders from whom he might receive admiration in return. These included whomever he deemed great in his status-filled world, such as politicians who would live in the White House, where he would be internationally aggrandized as a leading figure at the United Nations.

As Carver grew older, his therapeutic experience with me offered more accurate self-observation. By his junior year in college there were significant signs of change toward more normal narcissistic ambitions and relationships. He made friends with peers who were less status-conscious than those he formerly pursued. He finally felt liked for himself. Indeed, due to my persistent understanding of him, others also related to him positively because he had become capable of empathy and engaging others in a kinder way. This was a huge change. He also was developing a more realistic plan for his future which included an intent to study hard as always but with a goal of attending law school in preparation for more reasonably paced political aims.

His relationships with his parents also were changing. His connection with his father in particular was one of mutual respect. He also saw his mother more realistically with regard to her vulnerabilities observing a repetition of his former clashes with her being repeated with younger siblings. In general, remarkable progress was evident when he was more able to be observant of others' behaviors toward him without being reactive and impulsive.

My hope was that he would be able to live a life of introspection, leading to even greater self-acceptance for his true authentic traits and ambitions, without the need for the constant affirmation of others whom he idealized. He was no longer stuck metaphorically in Erik Erikson's (1950) second psychosocial stage of life: shame and doubt versus autonomy. This stage generally occurs from ages one-and-a-half to three. Psychosocial crises mean the conflicts between the needs of the self and the needs of society that Carver had been psychologically trapped in. Carver was learning to sustain a healthy balance between interest in himself and in others. That way, he could develop the intimate love relationship in marriage and the family he yearned for—along with his ambitions. Seeing the development of his grandiose self shifting into a more age-appropriate one that helped him to see the world and people in it in a less omnipotent and frightening way were goals of his treatment that were eventually realized.

This complex young man and his complicated treatment can be applied to others like him. The reader may relate to some of Carver or his parents' characteristics and not want to repeat his experiences with their own children. I hope that in reading about Carver (and the additional examples in the next few chapters), readers can recognize these characteristics in themselves and their children that *do* need to change and then use the information provided to create a healthier family life.

CHAPTER FIVE

The Romantic Narcissistic Mismatch

Clive and Laura

The story of Clive and Laura's courtship and marriage provides an example of how the narcissistic man is often joined in pathology by a partner in need of what his self-centeredness provides for her. They met in a laundromat near their apartments while in college and were married for thirty-five years. Clive was a true narcissist and from the beginning was attracted to Laura's empathic, impressionable, and trusting personality. After a handful of dates, he sought an exclusive relationship with her, due to his seeming adoration of her. This was the beginning of a manipulative relationship where Laura was led to believe she was exceptional in Clive's eyes, while he found in her the empath he needed to meet all of his demands for admiration and submission.

Actually, Laura was quite intelligent and capable. However, after years of paternal criticism and living with a narcissistic mother, she possessed a great deal of self-doubt. This prevented her from going to a superior college, because although she got accepted, she was fearful of leaving home and pursuing her talents. Unaware of her unconscious motivations, she attached herself to Clive—to *his* wishes and dreams, not hers.

Laura's mother put herself first. While a good homemaker, she was preoccupied with her appearance and was prone to addiction. Her father—a hard-working, blue-collar man—was often rude to his daughter. Unfailingly, Laura's mother let Laura know that her older brother was the more intelligent and promising child. These early family messages gave Laura a poor estimation of her abilities, so when she met Clive (the confident charmer who brilliantly took over any room and made himself the center of attention), she felt exceptional for the first time in her life. To feel part of that powerful façade was like magic to Laura, an acceptance and feeling of being uniquely desired that she hadn't experienced before. She accepted Clive's narcissistic needs just as she had accepted her mother's self-centered self-absorption.

Clive was the perfect example of the "golden child," created by two exceedingly doting parents. More than their favorite son (Clive had two younger brothers), they raised him in a way that taught him he had few peers in his world of excellence. This led them to provide their brilliant child with complex experiences, out of which came many notable and outstanding achievements. Both their parentage and his singular accomplishments led to his powerful sense of grandiosity. Clive's essential narcissism was grounded in his parents' own narcissistic needs. This contributed decisively to his need to create his own narcissistic web, which would include Laura.

As an emotional manipulator, he led and controlled Laura to join his journey to self-aggrandizement and infantile grandeur. It made her feel distinctly unusual to be his chosen one, given her brother's early superior talents that made her feel inferior. Clive's narcissistic traits made him an attractive choice to Laura, who was typically comfortable in the role of giving, sacrificing, and being passive. She felt at home with a person who knew how to take control. For his part, Clive felt drawn to her, as she was a partner who allowed him to feel strong, secure, in control, and dominant. She provided him with devotion, praise, and love that supported his need to be the center of attention, receive adoration, and be the leader of their partnership. She became the carrier of his greatness, at first *enjoying* his blatant conceit. Laura represented a decisive support for Clive by supplying him with a grand perception of his abilities. Clive felt whole in her presence.

Clive wanted to become the best personal injury lawyer in the market. He was successful. Indeed, outstanding work achievements are required by these characteristics of grandiosity and omnipotence, because such accomplishments involve self-focus, self-absorption, exhibitionism, and a tireless effort that often sacrifices or negatively impacts love relationships. To be famous, special, and attract attention becomes a way of life that is desperately sought after in order to find emotional connections. In other words, extraordinary talent is characteristically fueled by a desperate longing for human admirers who will validate it.

Clive's goals and standards were indeed those transmitted by his father. What he lacked was the ability to feel more than a fleeting sense of satisfaction from living up to his father's standards or reaching his goals. Only through the constant confirmatory approval of his externally admiring parents was he able to obtain a sense of heightened self-esteem. His growing-up years with his father severely disappointed him at times, as his father's work life as an acclaimed architect made him absent often. This resulted in Clive's desperate longing for his father's affection and affirmation that was only intermittently met. His mother's critical high standards and self-absorption added to his distress when his father was absent. Thus, he sustained a need for regular affirmation and approbation from others, which Laura filled naturally.

As his wife, Laura devoted herself to building his legal career with empathic acceptance. As a personal injury lawyer, her support may indeed have led to his tremendous success. In one case, he was acclaimed for making $6 million. In addition to her homemaking responsibilities, Laura was his bookkeeper and carefully organized his finances and appointments. She was enjoying her part in his work, for which she was more than capable.

However, there was a flaw in the way she viewed her husband: the highly successful lawyer. For a while, she saw the work he did for clients as altruistic, an interpretation important to her particular worldview. In time, however, her role as both his wife and his business partner led her to see that her husband saw his clients as money-making objects. She realized this after hearing him talk about his clients with disdain, never seeing them as people suffering from real loss.

With his great success, her bookkeeping was no longer as needed, and she ceased working for him when she gave birth to their twin boys. Devoted to her children, she went along with her husband's strivings to make these twin boys precociously stand out in their endeavors and follow his path to unique accomplishment. Capable and strong—and at Clive's insistence—they were enrolled in the most elite private school available. They excelled there, a fact that affirmed Clive's self-image as the superior father. The twins were a good match for their grandiose father, even though Laura had doubts about Clive's directing the twins to be involved in school leadership positions, rather than letting them just play and be themselves. She had always felt that children should have ample time to play, explore, and discover, but she kept these thoughts from Clive. The power of his personality, his persistent envy, and his view that his children had to be the best overwhelmed her sense of how she would raise her sons if given the opportunity. She diminished her own talents and became dependent on her husband and children's successes for her own sense of self-esteem—often doubting she was taking the right course for herself and her children. She just went along, concealing her dissatisfactions and worries about the twins' well-being. Even though her admiration of her husband's grandiose perfection was wearing a bit thin, she neglected her own admonitions in favor of pleasing him. By the time the twins were ten, it was too late to change their course of education.

To onlookers, Clive and Laura were the perfect match. They developed many casual friendships with others who admired their relationship and their enchanting children. Clive and Laura knew their roles: the narcissist leads and controls their dance, while the codependent follows and acquiesces, despite her self-doubts (Rosenberg 2013). He became known as an altruistic lawyer who was empathic to his clients, whom he served well. He traveled to indigent neighborhoods, seeking injured clients whose cases he knew would reap high financial gains. This made him look very compassionate, although his motives were pecuniary and expressive of his grandiosity.

Clive's essential narcissistic trauma was grounded in his parent's own narcissistic needs, which contributed decisively to him remaining immersed in their narcissistic web, a similar magnetic web that Laura would become immersed in. It was as if he was confronted with the task of achieving the wholesale internalization of a chronic narcissistic relationship with Laura, where she would fulfill his needed narcissistic supplies.

Laura remained the perfect entertainer in their home, like her mother. She always provided game nights, giving her husband center stage with his superior knowledge during games like Trivial Pursuit—even though it was her efforts behind the scenes that secured his popularity and success. She never complained of his long days of work, because she admired his supposedly selfless endeavors to help clients gain recompense for their injuries.

After twenty years of marriage, Laura began to find she was growing somewhat bored and annoyed by Clive's continuous regaling of his days at work, not only with her but with their couple acquaintances who were entranced by his success. She began to realize that she had suppressed her talents for the sake of her marriage, and she was becoming conscious that she, too, had ambitions and goals.

Clive and Laura also had a great deal of fun together and became confidants—or so Laura believed—continuously denying the one-sided nature of their sharing. He was humorous, knowledgeable about a wide range of subjects, and entertaining. Their marriage seemed successful, despite the occasional argument. However, if Laura didn't quickly accede to Clive's wishes, he would shut her out with an aggressive silent treatment and scowl. One of his dominant traits was that he wanted to be more continuously active than she did, in order to relieve his inner boredom and emptiness. She didn't perceive this accurately and assumed he had a vast array of admirable interests that he wanted to explore.

Laura was great at making friends, though they weren't always of the status that Clive desired. In any case, he always regaled new people with his life experiences, charming many couples young and old with his extensive achievements. Laura became increasingly conscious that she was tired of hearing his repeated stories and his need to be the center of attention, but she accepted this pattern with her role as the dutiful listener and admirer. Despite her growing frustration, she continued to be the pleaser and he, the controller. Plus, she continued to find him appealing, as he perpetually kept her attracted to his charm, boldness, confidence, and domineering personality.

When they had first met, she was delighted that Clive kept in almost constant contact with her throughout the day, texting and calling often. Over time, however, she began to feel he was more keeping her under his thumb than contacting her because he loved her. Unfortunately, Laura confused his controlling behavior with his loyalty and love for her. She began to feel used and underappreciated. One area of their life together that illustrates this was Laura's relationship with her children. Because she had more time to be with them, she was closer to them than was Clive, and he developed an almost continuous envy of their relationships. More empathic than Clive, Laura had more time to cultivate a nurturing connection with her boys, a fact that disgruntled and alienated him.

The false façade of the truly devoted husband was revealed to her most unexpectedly one day in the local supermarket when a man told her that Clive had been cheating on her. When Laura demanded to know the name of the lover, the stranger told her it was *his* boyfriend. This was the deepest, most devastating hurt and deception of her life, first because she learned that Clive was being unfaithful, then because she learned that he was gay—or, more accurately, bisexual.

Clive admitted the affair immediately when confronted. At first, Laura believed it was a one-time affair, but over several months she came to learn that there was at least one other.

Laura knew she would be lost unless she could get some help with this upending of her world, and she made contact with me for therapy immediately after learning the truth about her husband.

First, she began to understand that the truth about her husband's multiple affairs was responsible for their meager sex life—a situation she actually didn't mind and didn't question, desiring harmony in their marriage. In early sessions, she began to understand that she had sabotaged herself by choosing a partner whom she originally appreciated but eventually came to resent. Even though she was humiliated, enraged, and caught in a quagmire, she initially did not want to disrupt their rather perfect-seeming family life. She contained her vengeance and stayed with him, despite his admission of having extramarital affairs. Laura expected Clive to say more and explain his actions, thinking they could begin to create a rapprochement that could lead to a continuation of their partnership—albeit a weakened one. However, Clive said nothing new to explain or clarify his actions, further frustrating Laura. His lack of empathy for the impact his actions had on her was monumental.

When she began her individual psychotherapy, she began to strengthen her resolve to become more independent and knowledgeable and explore her talents. She experienced dual feelings of guilt in revealing her husband's flaws and pleasure in finally being able to find her own voice. He continued to manipulate her, promising he'd have no more affairs while showering her with gifts and appreciation. He did not want a divorce. She didn't, either, but was deeply conflicted, because she felt she had lived and was continuing to live a lie, which was very contrary to her high standards and values. He wanted his perfect-looking family and feared losing the love of his adult children—who by now were receiving accolades for their own achievements, which gratified him greatly.

During the first year after Laura's discovery of Clive's infidelities, her fear of being alone at this advanced stage of her life, her wish to

fix their marriage, and her comfort in the role of the endlessly loving, patient martyr became her plight. Clive refused to answer all
Laura's questions about his extramarital activities, which made her
feel slighted, angry, shut out, and confused, causing her to regress
emotionally. The result of this was an increasing inability to organize
her life. Her approach to every day was scattered, earmarked by losing
things and not knowing what to do next.

Laura's wishes to master her situation came into focus during her
sessions with me. My questions and comments helped Laura begin
to take an interest in developing ideas and activities that she could
declare were her own. She initiated an interest in learning more and
gaining skills. She also stated she wanted more time to herself, as well
as with friends that Clive felt were "below their status," but with whom
she felt comfortable.

In her therapy with me, Laura blamed Clive for his infidelities
while simultaneously praising him for his exceptional status as a lawyer. She did nothing to hurt his stellar reputation, despite all the harm
he had done to her. While she kept his secrets, she began (through
our therapy sessions) to realize that this was a manifestation of her
sacrificial nature, which had confused her into believing he loved her
reciprocally and mutually. One of Clive's behaviors that continued to
cause her confusion was the presentation of very expensive gifts, acts
that he assumed would calm her hurt feelings. She did enjoy them,
despite doubting their sincerity.

As her sessions with me continued, the clouds of confusion in
Laura's life began to clear, but they revealed a complex landscape that
initially defied her finding a correct path. While she was indeed desperately confused and angry, she was slowly becoming more self-reliant
and introspective. However, she was confused by what appeared to
her to be contradictory understandings, which made it difficult to
synthesize a plan for her future. It was through visiting and revisiting
these complexities in her life that we were able to establish an order
in her thinking that led her to become more self-confident. Her goals
and values were now taking center stage, although she continued to
struggle about a path to follow.

In Laura's therapy, power and control were a theme that she reenacted with me; it was an outlet for her to better express the power and control conflict she had with Clive. In therapy—in order to repair her feelings of vulnerability and narcissistic injury with her husband—she reversed roles with me: turned passive into active. She skipped sessions after my vacation, for example, struggling with my adult role of setting rules for therapy. She constantly questioned my regularly scheduled sessions and my timing of sessions, and even questioned if she should come to regular sessions or come at all, often leaving me with a sense of doubt about her plans similar to the way Clive had come to treat her. She wanted to keep the structure of therapy in flux so that no loss could be permanent—like the loss of the marriage she thought she had for decades. Although periodically introspective, she had trouble seeing how she was turning the therapy in part into a reenactment of the power and control Clive had over her; she was trying to have control over me, though unsuccessfully.

Laura never knew if Clive was still lying and cheating, and he silenced her questions after his initial revelations. She often silenced me by rambling—only periodically saying that she heard me, despite her talking. Other times, she would be purposefully quiet and focus on letting me talk. This rejected woman needed to take control somewhere in her life, and that was in the therapy room. She did not want marital therapy and did not want me to ever meet Clive, because our therapy time was her privilege and right; she should never again be violated in the way she had been violated by Clive. In time, she understood the rules and boundaries I set and abided by them, which successfully helped her feel and behave more in control, organized, sane, and focused in her external world. Actual boundaries in the therapy resulted in her being able to sustain boundaries in her daily life.

I was finally able to discuss with Laura her need for some reasonable power and control of her own, which led to a great deal of cognitive and affective inner confidence. She was able to control her intellectual understanding of her plight—even if she didn't want to change it, because of the prospective loss of the family unit she had built. Once the core of Laura's illusion (that I was more powerful than she) was understood, she could realistically and emotionally accept the disillusioning realities of her adult life. This gave her the real liberty she needed to choose her path going forward. After a year of therapy, with my support and interpretations, she had gained a great deal of inner strength and resilience and the prospect of pursuing her own ambitions and goals.

With my recommendation, Clive agreed to attend sessions with his own therapist. From what Laura related to me, Clive struggled from the start. For example, he bridled under the basic rules of therapy: that there was a specific end time and that his therapist had the right to take a vacation. Since he felt that he was always there for his clients, he believed he should receive the same regard and treatment from his therapist. He was not used to limits being imposed on him, and after a few months, he discontinued therapy. He was afraid to be dependent on someone he could not control.

The failure on Clive's part to continue in therapy became a powerful motivator for Laura to make a significant change in her life. Therapy for her husband had become her last hope that she could stay in an increasingly toxic marriage. Disappointed, saddened, and angry, she asked for a divorce; she realized she'd had enough.

The example of this marriage demonstrates how the damage done by the narcissistic man is not immediately clear-cut. Laura is an example of a woman without profound pathology who also has needs that she believes a "strong" man can satisfy. However, once in a relationship, this woman finds herself being pulled deeper and deeper down, only eventually finding the strength to get away from the anger and disappointment supplied by disloyal acts—like Clive provided Laura with in his infidelities.

Clive and Laura exemplify what psychotherapist Ross Rosenberg (2013) defines as emotional manipulation:

> Emotional manipulators interact with others from a perspective that is centrally focused on their needs. Their focus in relationships is usually on how people or situations impact them and their overwhelming need to be recognized and appreciated. Emotional manipulators typically exhibit an

unrealistic, inflated or larger than life view of their own talents while devaluing the contributions or abilities of others. They lack sensitivity and empathy in social situations and with individuals with whom they are in a relationship. (12)

He goes on to explain how manipulators and codependents are well-matched, a description that fits Clive and Laura well:

Codependents and emotional manipulators are naturally attracted to each other because of their perfectly compatible dysfunctional inverse personalities. In relationships, codependents are pathologically-oriented toward the needs of others while downplaying or ignoring the importance of their own needs. Emotional manipulators are pathologically-oriented toward their own needs while dismissing or ignoring the needs of others. Because codependents seek to care for the needs of others and emotional manipulators seek to have their needs met, they are well-matched relationship partners. . . . The same magnetic attraction force that brought them together also bonds them into a long-term and persistent relationship. . . . Because both are inherently emotionally and psychologically deficient, they share a distorted belief that the other will make them feel whole. Paradoxically, their dysfunctional relationship provides them both with a distorted sense of security and safety. For the codependent and the emotional manipulator, pain and safety are often fused together. (12–15)

This was Laura's plight, but with introspection and self-reflection in her therapy, she gained the insight that she could live her own fulfilling life with satisfaction and pride. Recognizing her own ambitions and goals, she was able to separate from Clive's rejections and proceed to create a life for herself that was more rewarding and gratifying.

An emotionally manipulative relationship may be similar to what you are experiencing in your own marriage. Like Laura did, you might want to consider seeking professional help. See chapter nine for a full discussion of how spouses of narcissists can live happy, healthy lives.

CHAPTER SIX

How a Couple Overcomes Narcissism

Wade and Ava

" am not a podiatrist!" Ava screamed as she tugged Wade's suitcase from the top of their bedroom closet. Usually the most talkative person in any room, Wade stood at the end of their bed, dumbfounded as he watched her flip open the top of the suitcase and point inside. "Put clothes in there now!" she demanded prior to stalking out of the room.

This was how Ava began to tell her husband, Wade, that she'd had enough. On their ride home from their neighbor's cocktail party, Ava came to the decision that her marriage to her narcissistic husband had to take a breather. He had to get out, or they would not survive as a couple.

Back at home in their bedroom, Wade finally found voice. "What did I do?" he called after her.

Ava was back in a flash. "What did you say when that idiot asked you if I was a *podiatrist*?"

"I said . . . uh . . . 'No, a pediatrician.' "

"And then . . .? I'll tell you," Ava hissed. "You said in your smirky way, 'Really no big difference, though.' And then the two of you had a good chuckle at my expense."

This had not been the first time that Ava, a hardworking and successful pediatrician, felt demeaned in public by her neurosurgeon husband, who felt that the work he did was the pinnacle of success in the world of medicine.

The description of the emotional manipulator/codependent couple by Rosenberg (2013) at the end of the last chapter applies to the case of Wade and Ava as well. However, as the interaction described above indicates, Ava is far less dependent on her narcissistic husband than was Laura. Like Laura, Ava desired her husband to be a strong, ambitious man, but when Wade's continuous narcissistic behaviors grew too much for her early in their marriage, she took action by telling him to get out for a while so that she could catch a break before continuing in a marriage she definitely wanted. He was shocked, because his narcissism was severely rocked for the first time in his marital life—and by the woman he loved.

I want to spend a little time describing who Wade and Ava were and how they came to be a married couple. It is important to remember that "the residue of each developmental phase is included in the next succeeding one, and simultaneously progressive elements foreshadow their later appearance, during the preceding developmental period" (Deutsch 1987, 22). I want you to keep this in mind as you see how each partner's growth emerged from early childhood to their adult lives together.

Wade's early life set the foundation for his narcissism. He was the crown prince of his family (being an only son) and was loved, pampered,

and indulged by his parents—particularly and especially his father. At
the age of one, however, Wade suffered a destructive yet formative
trauma: his parents divorced. They had met each other very young and
mutually agreed that they were not meant for each other over the long
haul. After the divorce, Wade's mother had limited contact with her
son, remarrying and dedicating herself to her new family. Thus, his
mother, whom he desired, left him alone with his doting father.

In their normal development, all children start from a narcissistic
stage in infancy, where they are the center of their mother's world.
As most children age, they come to learn that they are not the only
thing in their mother's life; they begin to develop a tolerance for having their natural narcissism modified, which then becomes a healthy
part of who they are.

This development did not happen for Wade, and he became stuck
in that infantile narcissistic stage out of which most children grow
naturally. Directly following his parents' divorce, Wade rarely saw his
mother, and he felt abandoned. His emotions stoked when he learned
she had remarried and quickly had other children. Whenever he saw
his mother in her new family—which was rare—he was hurt that she
cared so much for her other children and paid him practically no
attention at all. His mother's slight led to a deeper attachment to his
father, while also decreasing his mother's importance in his conscious
emotional life. This plays out years later in Wade's marriage to Ava,
as we shall see.

His father also remarried quickly, this time to a woman with two
daughters, both younger than Wade. Within a year, a third daughter
was born, and within two years, a fourth. In very short order, Wade
went from being the solitary and adored child to being one of five.

It is important to see Wade in this new family arrangement in
order to understand how the narcissism in his character developed
and strengthened. First, while now one of five, he was still the only
boy—the joy of a father who continued to indulge him. His father did
so because he felt guilt over his first failed marriage and, more importantly, because he saw Wade as very special, a boy who would grow up
to be outstanding in whatever field he decided to enter.

While they always lived together as a single-family unit, the parents and five children often seemed to be two families living *together but apart* under one roof. There was Wade and his father, and then there was his stepmother and the four girls. Wade's father was kind toward the girls, but it was clear that Wade was the star of his show. The stepmother, while supportive of his development, maintained some distance from Wade, because her attentions were much more directed at her daughters. They were treated with little kindness and forgiveness by their mother, who strictly expected them to listen to her dictates. If they did not, the consequences were hair-pulling, hitting, and punishments—all of which Wade escaped. In that sense, there was a male component of the family and a female component.

Wade was selfishly indifferent to his stepmother's treatment of his siblings because he felt so enmeshed with his father, whom he idealized. It was his father, who is here the guiding light in the plans and the aspirations of his son's development, that Wade endowed with a godlike status. It was because of his father's devotion to him—his dream of Wade's position in society, his love and belief in his son's future—that Wade continued to tolerate well the loss of his biological mother, denying the severe narcissistic insult of her abandonment. He consciously devalued her as unimportant in his life, because the emotional bond to his father was so significant. His father made him out to be so extraordinary and special, a belief that contributed to his becoming a celebrated neurosurgeon in the future.

Ava was the oldest of five children: three boys and two girls. Because her mother was a woman who was easily angered, Ava learned early to "keep her head down." A good daughter, she helped around the house, but her mother often flew into rages so that Ava preferred time alone in her small corner room. Her father was a hard-working factory foreman who always seemed exhausted at the end of his long days. A silent man for the most part, Ava knew little of him because he often fell asleep in front of the TV at night. The family had few resources, a situation that meant no designer clothes or fancy cars. They never took vacations together, so Ava's early memories of her family were always surrounding the mandatory sit-down dinners that often proceeded silently.

Ava was a hard worker, and the time she spent in her room was put to good use studying. She graduated salutatorian of her class, which meant she received a full scholarship to the state university, where she planned to pursue a pre-med curriculum. One of her early dreams was to be a pediatrician, and even though she had to support herself by working full time, she finished medical school on time.

Wade was four years older than Ava, and by the time she was in her internship, he was a fellow in neurosurgery at the major city hospital where he met her one day in the cafeteria. She was immediately impressed, maybe even overwhelmed, by this tall, handsome, successful, and extremely bright professional who was indeed the manifestation of the mate she had always dreamed of finding. Even though only in his early thirties, Wade had already established a reputation in his field that was growing wider than the hospital where they worked. And when they started dating, he proved himself a fount of knowledge about nearly everything, a quality that truly engaged Ava, because the only man in her early life had been a mostly silent father. When in company, Wade was always the most eloquently informed person in the room.

To her and to many others, it would have been a surprise to learn that Wade's path to this point in his life had been filled with trials. Wade's early experiences led him to develop behaviors that, on the surface, seemed to make him superlative, but were actually attempts to assuage deep and continuous pain. Due to his father's ongoing non-judgmental praise, Wade found himself always in need of being the smartest. An unintended consequence of this was that Wade developed habits that resembled attention-deficit hyperactivity disorder (ADHD), the need to be constantly learning about everything—but in ways that had no structure or boundaries. This hyperactive behavior also kept Wade from ever contemplating his feelings surrounding the loss and abandonment of his mother.

As a college undergraduate, he pursued pre-med but struggled—not because he was not intellectually bright enough but because his approach had taken on the scattered and disorganized style of his early "learning about everything." In effect, he had poor focus. While he did graduate on time with a major in pre-med, his record was mediocre. He was accepted into a second-rate medical school where he immediately ran into trouble, flunking out at the end of the first year.

This disappointment did not, however, deter Wade. It actually acted as a spur to his ambition, and he found a medical school that allowed students to proceed at their own pace. This fit Wade well, and he excelled to the point that he was accepted into a prestigious residency in neuroscience. This led to his fellowship as a neurosurgeon, meaning he had overcome his initial failure through his own dint of effort, which only added to his narcissism.

Let's return to Wade and Ava in their marital life. They had trouble enjoying each other's accomplishments as a neurosurgeon and a pediatrician. Wade viewed himself and his surgical prowess as much more accomplished and complex than Ava's pediatric work—despite her impressive academic journey on her own steam. He viewed her lesser income and more flexible hours with disdain, not appreciating the lengths she went to in supporting the families she took care of (including their own).

Since the time they met when she was an intern and he, a fellow, Wade had forgotten the 100-hour work weeks of her internship and didn't appreciate the exhaustion Ava felt. She, however, overlooked this because she was drawn to his evident brilliance, interest in learning a wide range of subjects, and vigorous yet difficult attempts to complete his medical goals, which he did with the aforementioned prolonged years of study.

As noted, coming from a poor background where she had to independently finance and carry out her medical training, she was impressed by the support Wade received from his family during his extensive and extended training. He, in contrast, devalued Ava's great accomplishments, kind nature, and empathy to her patients. She even made home visits—unheard of in today's contemporary medical world.

Wade's need for admiration was extensive. His self-absorbed career goals and ambitions kept him from caring about developing a relationship with his children when they were young, which he would later regret and try to address. He envied his wife's relationship with the children but didn't understand, for example, how his walking in the house after work talking on the phone and ignoring the children's need for his attention was unempathic. His self-absorption held sway; they could wait for his attention after he took care of his own needs. In a way, he was unknowingly mimicking his biological mother's abandonment of him in the way he treated his children.

He wished he lived in a more exclusive neighborhood, because he wanted his children to attend a more elite school that would reflect well on him. It was his need for recognition, rather than his kids' education, that led to this desire. His wife did not share these standards, given her background, to his *never-ending* chagrin. Status was clearly more important to him than to her, and he never let her forget it.

Ava's demand for a temporary separation cited at the start of this chapter flabbergasted Wade. He was amazed she could stand up on her own like that, despite his protest. Unconsciously, this separation reminded him of the loss of his biological mother, but he was consciously unaware of that. Ava was certain this was a path she needed to explore, and he moved out, living in an apartment for six months until she said he could come home. During that time, she hired a child minder to help with their children while she worked. She also spent time deciding how to strengthen their marriage into more of a reciprocal relationship.

During adolescence, Wade and Ava's children began having difficulties in their education. In his grandiose style, Wade decided he was going to take over. He realized he had not been a "present" parent when they were younger, so it was now incumbent upon him to make matters right. His sense of right was all wrong, however. Immediately, he began interfering with their independence as they did their schoolwork. He saw no harm in even doing their homework for them and, in fact, cheating their way into better grades. Of course, this didn't teach them what they needed to learn but gave them a sense of dependence on his control over them. Ava never relented in protesting his actions and educational attitude, which confused the growing children's values. As they grew to college age, he kept very close ties with them on the phone, answering their calls immediately—even if it disturbed his medical work—and continuously texting them. He had no idea that this was detrimental to their appropriate developing autonomy, and it infuriated Ava, whose diminishing control over the children she had principally raised was now in jeopardy. His self-absorption led him to view his children as extensions of himself, like his medical practice, and he excluded his wife—unless he needed her to provide the homemaking chores that complicated her intense working life. She remained the caretaker both at work and at home, while he excelled in his medical practice to his great self-satisfaction and external acclaim. Their sexual life was minimal, because she lost interest in him due to his self-absorption and need for admiration. She did recognize his accomplishments, which he didn't reciprocate—despite her outstanding medical practice and her recurring threats of another separation. Her values of promoting independence in her children competed with his wish for control of them. This was an unending source of conflict.

Ava was growing stronger and more decisive about her values. Because she wanted her children to remain in an intact family, she decided she would never seek a divorce. But her situation continuously filled her with rage that she handled by walking out on Wade periodically. One strategy she used was going to plays alone to find some peace of mind; this helped her avoid exploding emotionally. One eventful weekend, she went to a spa on her own, which demolished Wade's sense of self-importance. He could not understand her wish to have her own needs met even if it meant getting them alone. She began to prefer her own company to their partnership. The children allied themselves at different times with each parent, depending on who gave them what they wanted. These children were overindulged by their father, who was raising narcissistic, self-absorbed children who expected him to spend extraordinary amounts of money supporting their self-centered interests.

Because Wade's narcissism demanded that he never be alone and unoccupied, he had a constant need for activity; being alone meant he had to experience his feelings and emptiness.

Ava suggested they begin marital therapy with me during the children's adolescence. He immediately displayed grand gestures in the therapy room. He would literally take over the room, draping his large coat and stethoscope over the couch and repetitively talking—excluding Ava's voice from being heard. This led to Ava's preference for individual sessions for each of them.

The individual sessions improved their marriage significantly, as Wade learned to include Ava's wishes in the extensive, expensive outings that he arranged without her consent. These outings were a constant source of contention. He changed his behavior to include her desires but didn't understand why this mattered. If he wanted to go somewhere, he assumed she would too. He didn't understand the meaning behind including her in his plans but just followed my recommendations to improve his marital relationship. He faulted his wife for her needs and found her to be the "crazy" one who might want to relax on a weekend, rather than scurry around continuously attending concerts, movies, plays, or museums. A great marital struggle continued, and he hoped his therapy with me would help him regain some equilibrium in this troublesome family situation.

Both from Ava's accounts and his own descriptions, people outside the family were beginning to react negatively to Wade's narcissistic behaviors. At work, where he was exceedingly admired, he often spent an inordinate amount of time dominating the office, regaling his staff with his daily life when they needed time to do their work. He had no awareness of the impact of this inappropriate behavior. A second result was that he was always behind and disorganized in his medical paperwork.

However, he was competitively sought after as a surgeon. Being sought after of course buoyed his need for admiration, and he worked endlessly though scattered hours to prove his worth and gain his wealth. This further alienated Ava, who held to her decision to keep the family intact, even though she was excluded from his daily life (except for the time he spent telling her in detail about his medical practice while ignoring hers). He also didn't understand that his perpetual storytelling in mixed company bored and excluded others; he believed that his status still made him a welcome guest. His lack of self-awareness was appalling to his empathic wife.

It is noteworthy, as mentioned above, that Wade's symptoms resembled an ADHD. In his medical practice and at home, he demonstrated disorganization of his medical records and finances, distractibility, impulsivity, inattention to others, and deviance from the norm with his hyperactivity level. However, symptoms alone are not reliable indicators of a diagnosis. His scattered behavior—which disturbed Ava tremendously—was out of his awareness.

The ability to admit to problems and perceive his own part in them presupposes a relatively well-developed internal sense of self, which was lacking. His sense of self was more dependent on outside approval. His near-total denial of his past poor school performance, for example, was a narcissistic defense that he used because he could not tolerate admitting he was not good at something. In his therapy, he continuously reminded me that he did persevere in his over-extensive medical training. This furthered his grandiosity, because he did overcome many obstacles—no matter how many universities and how long it took to meet his goals.

Ava brought up in her therapy how striking it was that Wade was incapable of being alone. This accounted for his over-controlling influence on his adolescent children, whom he kept in overly close contact with, texting and talking to them daily. Even at night when he had time to be with Ava, he preoccupied himself with surfing the web to avoid any lurking feelings under this continuous activity.

Further, Wade had to be well-planned on every excursion they took together and account for every moment, regardless of Ava's needs, in order not to feel his insecurities. He experienced extreme separation anxiety when he was not with his wife or teenagers or working.

His deficit lay in his inability to experience a full range of feelings without needing to either act on them immediately or to deny them via defensive activity. Only by knowing his feelings would it be possible for him to know if he should act on them. His continuous actions and diversions, along with his lack of objective self-awareness, were an avoidance of interpersonal stress and conflict and the full range of feelings that come with muddling through to actual intimacy.

Along with Wade's disturbed self-esteem regulation, his disorder of narcissism was evidenced by his need for admiration and attention. Wade was more vulnerable than he appeared and more dependent on outside approval than he could admit. What seemed most prominent were his narcissistic vulnerabilities. He could not tolerate that he didn't know everything. If someone else was ignorant, which he was quick to observe, that was okay—if it was not him. Others could be devalued but not him. He often insisted that whatever he did was the right thing, even when objectively it was not.

His overt symptoms of ADHD were a real behavioral defensive cover for his narcissistic temperament and vulnerable self-esteem. It is important to think of his ADHD symptoms as operating to maintain an emotional status quo in his mode of relating to the world. What makes the construct of narcissistic pathology of special value in organizing these varied defenses is the way it focuses attention on Wade's efforts to maintain self-esteem, especially the avoidance of those feelings that would threaten it, and the impact these efforts had upon how he managed his relationships.

A robust, tall, heavy-set man, Wade looked prominent. In therapy, he extolled and idealized his family of origin—including his stepmother and father, despite their major flaws in child-rearing that consequently brought hardships, which he ignored. At the same time, he disparaged Ava's impoverished background, despite the accomplishments of her adult siblings, who had overcome much adversity. Ava, too, was attractive: a tall, slender woman whom he didn't have high enough regard for or understand. He never appreciated that she was sought after by community groups.

What held them together in the long run? They both believed in being faithful partners. Despite their ever-constant disagreements, they loved their children deeply, and they held family life sacred.

Like many narcissistically led duos, they loved each other, cared for each other's well-being (to the extent that Wade was capable), and—with therapeutic intervention over many years—accepted each other's flaws and anxieties. Wade was a loyal provider and husband, even though his empathy for Ava was so faulty. She in turn was used to being sacrificial and had a stunning sense of humor that withstood the depreciation he held for her.

This couple's therapy led to some real changes.

For Ava, she was able to open up about her past, her difficult childhood, and her struggles to become a successful pediatrician. In addition, with my help, she was able to communicate to Wade her frustrations with his narcissistic behaviors. She understood that she carried the emotions in the family and continued to receive therapeutic support while he disengaged from his therapy; he had to keep his emotional guard up for fear of seeing his weaknesses.

Wade also improved, although his positive development was somewhat grudgingly made. In time, he included Ava in planning the extensive outings he loved to go on, even though he never really comprehended that they represented a way to avoid being alone with his difficult thoughts.

Most notably, as stated above, this couple that started with such difficulties learned to stay together and strengthen their relationship. His somewhat contemptuous and controlling attitude toward me lessened as his therapy proceeded when he found that my insights improved his relationship with his wife.

The behavioral gains he made in therapy—such as learning to include his wife in making their frequent travel plans and letting her relax while he went off in multiple directions, not to miss out on any attraction that would increase his self-esteem—salvaged their recreational time together and appeased her needs for recognition. He was learning how his behavior affected her. She came to appreciate these changes in his behavior, even though she knew he didn't understand the meaning behind them. He was often following instructions like they were a script he had learned, because he cared for her happiness in the end—even if he didn't comprehend her actual needs.

Ultimately, Wade's genuine capacity for love of Ava improved and kept him in tow, so to speak. This allowed her needs to be expressed more fully, even if Wade didn't want to acknowledge their importance.

As her therapy progressed, Ava became more open to Wade about the adversities in her life that she had overcome growing up, and he came to appreciate these victories over her traumatic past. He often lapsed into his narcissistic self-absorption only to find that she then went off physically and psychologically on her own, excluding him from her activities if she needed to. She used to run away from the household without keeping in contact with him or explaining her whereabouts, which had a significant impact on his inability to tolerate being alone, but her behavior changed. She began to clearly tell him her needs and where she was going to satisfy them and carry out her autonomous plans. He came to realize that Ava's alone time was a fact of their marriage if he wanted it to work, which he did.

Therapy helped Ava separate from her early dependence on her husband, derived from growing up in her family of origin that lacked both financial and emotional support. She managed to acquire, over the course of her treatment, a maternal protector in her therapist to stand between Wade's and her needs. As noted above, her mother had been a very overwhelmed, self-centered, rageful, aggressive woman, which perhaps led Ava to marry Wade, who also was self-centered but not aggressive. Further, Wade became more capable of nurturance over time, especially after my therapeutic intervention. His frantic fear of Ava running away (like his biological mother) showed her that he loved her and worried about her, an experience that she did not have with her mother.

Wade resented Ava's newfound independence because it made him feel less of the admired center of her life. However, he had to keep her desires in mind more now, if they were to enjoy and sustain their relationship. He finally gave some credence to her hobby, jewelry-making, that she was gaining pecuniary rewards from by selling in museum shops. Wade came to recognize she needed and deserved admiration for her entrepreneurship, artistic talent, and creativity—things he had previously devalued as insignificant. To get the love she needed from Wade, Ava had to become more narcissistic herself—in a healthy way. In the therapeutic emotional climate, she became accustomed to feeling understood. To receive love from her husband in the way she needed, she had to develop more self-love. The way to gain his admiration was to see herself as a truly superior person—as Wade saw himself.

This was indeed a satisfactory outcome for Ava and Wade. Self-regard or self-esteem, self-interest, and self-regulation are central to human development. In my view, this couple's interest in themselves and in each other were eventually no longer polar opposites but omnipresent and intricately interconnected, generating both conflict that continued to be resolved with mutual enhancement and vitality—in each individually and as a marital couple.

The outcome for Ava and Wade was very different from that of Clive and Laura. The resolution of their differences and difficulties took a very different course. If you identify with their plight, the option of marital therapy that is arranged with individual sessions for each is one to consider. See chapter nine for more suggestions.

CHAPTER SEVEN

The Wish and Fear of Exploiting Others—The Use of Empathy with a Narcissistic Man

Rio

R io was a retired older man who was struggling with the decision to leave his young spouse of fifteen years for multiple sexual liaisons. In his sixties, he was not interested in exploring his whole life (as is common in psychotherapy) but in my helping him make a decision about whether to leave his long-term partner, whom he found deficient in buoying up his sense of self. His belief that multiple sexual conquests would benefit him is certainly in line with any definition of narcissism. However, that he was coming to me so that I could tell him such a plan was okay proves that he was an example of a man whose narcissism was not all empowering. Otherwise, he would have simply gone about his plan to leave his spouse and have sexual affairs.

When I realized he was not interested in examining his life to better understand the predicament he was finding himself in—that he only wanted me to validate the decision to leave his spouse for a lineup of younger women—I decided to simply focus on my empathy for him in the hope that he would struggle forward to a better sense of who he was. This older man's aging and retirement from work were, in themselves, narcissistically wounding, so my empathy became an indispensable tool—enabling him to see his true self partially expressed and safeguarded at the same time.

Rio had a fifteen-year-long marriage with a previously divorced woman, Eli, who was ten years younger than he. She had two grown children. Eli was of Swedish origin, physically stunning in his estimation and smart, but she spoke English with a Swedish accent, which unsettled him. He trusted her because she was kind and giving, but the relationship was largely platonic; he was not sexually attracted to her, due to her accent and mediocre work life. These characteristics made him feel somewhat foreign and superior to her, which meant that she couldn't fulfill his needs for fully mirroring and aggrandizing his self-absorbed sense of self. He held no interest in her two adult children.

What was of total concern to Rio when he came to me was his indecision about leaving Eli. On the one hand, he felt he was exploiting her because he was not leaving her at a time when she did not love him; he was taking advantage of her kind and giving nature. In truth, she cared for him deeply.

What had prevented Rio from leaving her, however, was not some moral compunction; rather, he feared how others would view him for leaving his wife to have sexual relationships with other young women. He did not want to appear to be exploitative—although that indeed was what he wanted to be, in that he hoped for multiple relations with other women whom he did not have to care for in any deeply intimate or reciprocal way. Any attempt on my part to help him explore the impact his actions would have on Eli (should he leave her) or on the multiple women he hoped would desire him left him feeling I wasn't concentrating fully on him. He actually said, "Me, me, me," in more than one session when I attempted to discuss the effects that his actions would have on the women in his life. He had originally hoped that Eli's young age would satisfy his needs for accolades by a young lover, but her inadequacies (in his estimation) diminished that hope. Her children were a further hindrance to his desire for her, because he couldn't tolerate her divided interest in him and the children—with whom he was totally detached.

He was a successful financial planner and commodities trader who made millions of dollars in his forties due to his clever investments, which gave him a sense of security for the first time in his life. His mother, with her constant debts, had warned him to be extremely careful about choosing to marry and to make a lot of money through hard work. His father had basically abandoned the family and given him no alternative views. He followed his mother's instruction to the letter, doing work that he didn't find fulfilling but did secure his position in the community and give him endless resources to support himself and the woman with whom he lived. He feared loneliness—a reason to keep the connection with his partner—but this didn't offer him enough incentive to stay with her.

He didn't understand or seem to care that multiple relations, should he find them, might leave him feeling sought after but empty over time, due to the lack of real, authentic mutual ties. Power was much more important to him, and he ostensibly was only interested in his present pleasures, not his future. He felt that speaking of his future with me meant his immediate needs weren't being understood. Speaking of his future also forced him to think of his aging, which he wanted to deny because it was so narcissistically wounding.

As an independent businessman, he led an unstructured life, maintaining his investments as his major occupation. He had some recreational interests and some male companions he enjoyed spending time with, but he trusted no one, believing that the basis of life's morality was one of an existence where you give to someone in return for them giving something back to you. He didn't believe people really cared for one another in a deep and enduring way; instead, he believed they were manipulated and exploited to sustain relationships that gave them some kinds of benefits. This was his entrenched worldview.

To illustrate how Rio's narcissism interfered with the real relationships in his life, the example of his best friend sheds some light. This man was in Rio's opinion a strikingly intelligent friend in need, whom he financially sustained. In sessions with me, Rio told me he supported this friend not because he thought of himself as a generous man but because he felt this man was brilliant and understood him. He was Rio's equal. Though Rio didn't understand it, this friendship was illustrative of what he really needed: a mutually reciprocal relationship where there was give and take between them. Despite his financial support for this man, Rio told me he was not helping him because he was generous; he was helping because of what the man could give him in return: enlightened discussions. These discussions validated Rio's sense of his own intelligence and high regard, something Rio needed unendingly. Indeed, these were significant virtues and valuable assets in a relationship, but to Rio they only represented the concrete needs he had that this man gave him in return for his support.

I tried to validate—that is, understand—his points of view (even if I didn't agree with him) to show him I was trying to grasp and process his logic. He didn't understand mutual relationships, only believing insistently and deeply in the exploitation and manipulation of one person for another. As his therapist, I believed I was also someone like this male friend, whom he paid to receive unending validation.

Given this questionable morality, one would think he would easily leave his spouse. Or that he would simply have affairs with other women. What stopped him was a fear that others would find out, maybe seeing him out in public with a woman or hearing about it from another friend. If so seen, he feared he would be viewed as a "creepy guy." In other words, the view others held of him was the only view he could have of himself. Several times, he compared himself to disgraced politicians, not only for their sexual antics but for getting caught at what they did.

In therapy, he wanted me to reassure him that his exploitation of women was permissible in our society and in fact the norm. Any talk of actual mutual satisfactions from a male-female relationship he felt was naïve on my part. He disputed that I could possibly be as altruistic as he believed I thought I was, although I never gave him that impression directly. It was his idealization of me that led him to this point of view. He argued with me incessantly that altruism did not exist; however, as I did not take a stand either way, he was actually arguing with himself. I was just an object, so to speak, to have a dialogue with. He invented me as a kind of moral person with the kind of high moral character he viewed as gullible and foolhardy.

He needed this illusion of me so that he could carry out dialogues with me that validated his position. But he rarely felt satisfied with our talks, because I wouldn't give him direct advice. Even if I had, he wouldn't have trusted it, because he ultimately trusted no one—even though he purported to trust me. Why would he trust me and continue to speak with me if I continually disappointed his wishes for direct advice? His reasoning was that I was an expert in human relations, something he knew little about (which was true). My imperfections were based on his projections that I was a limited human being, as all humans are, but existed in my therapeutic role solely to serve him, which was due to his belief that, in fact, my job was to serve him and meet the needs that he was entitled to, because he was paying me.

He had some notion that I might also care for him, but he couldn't resolve that question. He completely denied his own subjectivity, only ascribing such motivations to me. He believed he was objective in attributing to people traits of limited character and integrity. I saw my role as trying to understand him so that he could understand and accept himself. This was a kind of validation where I needed to hold his opinions nonjudgmentally, without inserting my reactions of right or wrong. This allowed us to remain connected, talk, and explore his life without descending into a win-or-lose debate. This type of validation was my attempt to communicate feedback that said, "I understand you as yourself." I was respecting that what he believed held validity for him, and I was trying to understand it (if not agree with it).

My only hope was that empathy could be curative if I could enter into Rio's thoughts, feelings, and hopes accurately. In our therapy sessions, he often retold his train of thought, which became very repetitive but seemed to be what he was after. True empathy is learning the other's point of view, which I took as my aim when we were not resolving his question of whether to tell his mate he wanted to be unfaithful. If I attempted to be objective, I was not viewed as empathic; this disappointed and enraged him because of his frustration with my having my own points of view.

In psychoanalytic terms, this meant that I had to have an experience-near perspective, only focusing on what he was trying to tell me, not an objective experience-far perspective, where explanations are given. He even began to tell me what he wanted me to say, a kind of word-for-word mirroring, as if he could give me a script that would not frustrate him. I actually did mirror his thinking occasionally, giving him verbal and nonverbal recognition that said, "I see you as yourself." It was as if without my word-for-word reflection, he couldn't see himself in my response. However, my mirroring didn't really work; when I attempted to do this, he became frustrated that I was not telling him what I really knew and only parroting his words. There was no resolution to this conundrum.

Beyond mirroring and validating him, I also tried to feel his internal workings. Although I may not have shared the experiences he felt, I could imaginatively try to project myself into his reality and emotional state. That is, I had to extend my imagination emotionally into his shoes in order to sustain an empathic connection with him.

Only periodically did what I say feel enough to him. There was no way out of this dilemma. My dismay derived from the pressure I felt to suspend any of my own points of view to show my respect for his vantage points, only to find if I did so then he felt I was holding back what he needed to learn from me. I hoped if I was sufficiently empathic, he would feel understood, as well as feel that he existed in his own right, capable of coming to his own decision (Kitron 2011). This was my reasoning in not giving him advice, which he would only question and doubt. My greatest hope was to promote his capacity for autonomous thinking. I further thought that if he could not articulate more fully what he wanted from me, my own mental state and visceral reactions to Rio might alert me to what he unconsciously needed (Kitron 2011).

I suspected that it was important to Rio that he could be distressed in my presence and that I could forbear these episodes in a way no one else had ever done before. When distressed in front of others in the past, he had been confronted by people who reacted strongly to his behavior. I was not going to respond in that way, because I wanted to be a holding environment for him at a difficult time—a place where he would feel safe.

I wondered if his wish for sexual conquests expressed a need for power. I was hoping that if I did not judge him in this area, I would be able to help him begin to articulate the meaningfulness of such actions (should he follow through on them). During these discussions, I became aware that his idealized view of me contained the good parts of him and that his belief in the "do for me, and I'll do for you" world were the bad parts of him. I hoped that in time he would be able to satisfy his relationship desires with a woman who would give him more self-contentment (Grant and Harrari 2011).

Rio seemed to be a man who had been deprived of a healthy balance of unconditional loving relationships as a child. Deprived of such narcissistic supplies, I believed he suffered deep narcissistic wounding. He was the son of a mother whose maternal interaction impeded his ability to internalize a sense that being himself was unconditionally good, trustworthy, and special just for being himself. Lacking this formative experience growing up, he could not entertain this view as an adult and lived a kind of empty life—a life that he obsessively tried to fulfill with shallow relationships. He desperately needed continued narcissistic supplies of an external nature in order to build a self-image that countered his highly unsatisfying retirement and a marriage he felt was deeply flawed. He was a man who felt diminished and sought from me relief from that experience and a refuge from his anxiety and turbulent inner life. As we concluded his therapy, he had begun to realize his choices were not up to me. He remained the master of his own decisions. Like the other narcissistic men in this study, he needed external validation that could never be sufficiently satisfied because he lacked a core sense of self-worth.

CHAPTER EIGHT

Dale and Her Narcissistic Father

The narcissistic father is a self-absorbed man who sees his children as extensions of himself. He is unable to emotionally separate himself from others in his family. He always expects his children to meet his parental expectations, regardless of their feelings and needs. He has little ability to see his children or wife as individuals in their own right. He expects that he is the king of the house and his kids and spouse should anticipate his needs and strive to fulfill them—even if he doesn't make them clear. He expects family members to know him well enough to read his needs without his explaining them; it is their job to nourish him. Further, the narcissistic father expects empathy from others but cannot reciprocate. He expects others to drop what they are doing when he makes a request (Brown 2008).

In the myth of Narcissus, there is another character, Echo, who stands behind Narcissus and, having lost her ability to form her own words, repeats the utterances of others. She falls in love with Narcissus and follows him, hoping he will say loving words that she can repeat back to him. But Narcissus is so taken with his own self-love that he is unable to hear her. Unable to capture his attention or love, she dies. This story is the template for the narcissistic parent who cannot see, hear, or react to the needs of another—including his child, who is represented by Echo. According to Pressman and Donaldson-Pressman (1994), this is an allegory for the narcissistic family, where the narcissistic parent's needs are focused on, rather than the child's independent functioning.

Children raised by at least one narcissistic parent can develop many physical and psychological problems. In her book *Children and Narcissistic Personality Disorder: A Guide for Parents* (2015), Bailey-Rug describes several (iii, iv):

- Low self-esteem
- A sense of heightened responsibility for others
- Anger turned toward the parent with the narcissistic personality disorder
- Anger turned inward, sometimes with self-harming behaviors
- Depression
- Anxiety
- Complex post-traumatic stress disorder
- A sense of being the victim of an abuser
- Inflammatory disorders

Dale was the only child of a narcissistic father. Growing up, she was generally reclusive, spending most of her time outside of school with her father. He had a way of secluding her from outside influences. She was responsive to his expectations; if she couldn't meet them, she felt a sense of failure. Dale spent her life doing what she thought her father expected in order to gain his love and approval. Consequently, she did not develop a secure sense of self.

She always believed it was her job to make her father feel better about himself. He often confided in her about marital and work problems, topics he should have shared with his wife or another adult. If he was upset, she worked hard to make him happy, trying to be the perfect child and never upset him.

Dale's father could subtly show his disapproval. He wasn't openly threatening, but his body language spoke to her. He would give her a disgruntled look or turn his back on her whenever he deemed she had not responded to his needs fully enough. His specific tone of voice could shift and feel threatening. He also used silent treatment toward her when she inadvertently didn't please him, which caused her pain and confusion. She experienced guilt for angry feelings toward him, at times, that she didn't understand. Always wanting to please him, she thought it was her fault if she didn't. Thus, there were confused boundaries between father and daughter, defining when she was and wasn't responsible for his feelings, actions, and beliefs. If she had a differing point of view from him, she felt selfish.

All her own accomplishments felt somehow unreal, as if all she attained by herself was tenuous. This underlay her fragile sense of self and vulnerability to criticism or imagined slight. She needed his attention and affirmation of her own accomplishments to feel they were permissible.

However, when she turned fifteen, she wanted her own life with her peers outside the family. This meant she couldn't always be available when her hard-working father wanted something from her, which began, for the first time, to cause endless arguments. She was trying in a healthy way to develop a stable sense of self as an adolescent not always needing his approval. Part of this process for her was learning to tolerate her guilty feelings for not constantly attending to his needs. This required that both she and her father develop the ability to tolerate change in their relationship, so her growth was not stultified.

Adolescence represents a time when the individual is transitioning from external to internal sources of approval. This was Dale's conundrum.

Until now, Dale was perceived by her father as the child who was always by his side, supporting his needs, giving him praise, and viewing him as the best father ever. She had perceived that she existed for his benefit, was there to calm his angry emotions after work, and was always prepared to make him snacks when he was hungry. She was a parentified child. That means she was the parent and he, the child in their pathological role reversal.

Now entering middle adolescence with a growth in her cognitive abilities, she was able to see herself and her father more accurately. Not relying as much on his love and appreciation, however, left her with fewer consistent sources of self-esteem. She could feel more emotionally unstable and less certain about who she was.

This effect of the father's narcissism on the family was subtle. There was no overt dysfunction. To an outsider, the family relations looked healthy. Dale came across as a well-functioning teenager with a strong outer shell protecting a soft and more vulnerable inner core. There was no expressed anger—or much expression of any other emotion. She wasn't ignored, but the reality was that she sacrificed her needs for her father's. Anything that disturbed him was not to be tolerated but addressed. Although she wasn't overtly mistreated, she could not call on him for her own emotional support. The need of this parent was the focus of the family, and Dale was a cardboard cutout of the good-and-successful child.

The problems did not appear until Dale wanted to assert herself and make her own emotional demands on the family. Only when she began to compare herself to her peers, a critical passage from early to middle adolescent development, did she begin to understand that there was something wrong with her relationship with her father.

Prior to her adolescence, Dale was an excellent student and athlete who never made mistakes or showed poor judgment that might negatively reflect on her father. She felt this helped her consistently be an excellent student and basketball player, as her father had been when he was growing up. He coached her in basketball for years, and she excelled. Dale didn't consider if this was her interest; her only aim was to please her father. He regularly played with her in the yard at their basketball court, perfecting her skills. She was expected to drop what she was doing with her peers at any moment to have an extra practice—if he felt she needed it—in order to remain the stellar player he expected her to be. Now, however, as she moved from early to middle adolescence and internally separated from her father, her need to please herself and her friends increased, and her need to please her father decreased.

Healing from isolation is not an easy venture. Dale had no other siblings to share her reverse parenting burden. As an only child, she had been expected to live up to her father's demands and expectations academically. As a very bright youngster, she gained his favor and adoration with her straight As and awards for excellence in math and science. This brought him great satisfaction, as he was the research scientist and head of his neuroscience department at the local science laboratory. He expected Dale to follow in his footsteps, which she did. As *he* studied genetics, he expected her to do the same, and she did, even though there wasn't a course for that in her high school. He tutored her on the subject, and again, she excelled. They had many fascinating discussions of genetic research that she enjoyed at the time without realizing this was keeping her from healthy relationships with her peers. Her life was narrow, involving mostly this father-daughter relationship. But the job of parenting her father was becoming too much for her.

As noted, the difficulties came when she wanted more independence from him when she became an adolescent striving for autonomy. She was pleased with her successes and appreciated and misconstrued what appeared to be his doting on her, even though it was mostly selfish on his part. But when it came to her wishes to be independent, make her own plans with her friends, and enjoy fashioning her own appearance, he rather harshly objected. He complained that he was entitled "as her father" to continue directing all her activities. Where once his views were most highly valued, she was now beginning to turn to friends.

Dale's mother was passive and went along with her husband's dictates. She, too, functioned as his empath, allowing for his dominance in their life. He was the senior parent in their household—until Dale began to complain to her mother during puberty. Her mother, fearing her husband's rage, held her daughter back from expressing her growing needs for autonomy. However, by age fifteen, Dale's mother lost her grip on her daughter's behavior. While frustrated at times, she began to understand Dale was changing in a healthy way. When Dale's father saw his wife side with Dale, he got angry, feeling personally injured by his wife and daughter for colluding against him. Thus, marital disputes paralleled father-daughter disputes. Dale's father took any opposition as a personal affront. He was used to controlling his department at work and, heretofore, his wife and daughter at home.

Dale was changing. In fact, she was developing a crush on a boy who played baseball; she wanted to learn that game so she could support him. This disturbed her father greatly, because her focus on baseball took her away from concentrating solely on basketball. He planned on basketball giving her a scholarship to college and meeting his needs for control of her. In effect, he was trying to socially isolate her so that she would stay in his control. This father-daughter relationship made him feel powerful.

Dale deeply internalized her father's disappointment in her. One of the most troubling effects of reverse parenting is a heightened emotional susceptibility for the child. Taking on the parent's feelings—usually negative feelings like disappointment—and integrating them is difficult, and children are often unable to release them (Brown 2008). Dale's psychological boundaries had not been sufficiently strong as she was growing up, so she was not able to filter out and choose which of her father's emotions she wanted to accept and which to disagree with. Consequently, at fifteen, she was becoming *unreasonably* guilty if she did not meet all her father's dictates. She remained vigilant of signs that he was disappointed in her and feared his reactions. She became increasingly anxious when she couldn't let go of the feelings that he induced in her. She suddenly began to have panic attacks when she feared his disapproval.

Regarding her athletics, she began to recognize that he thought he was her personal coach. For the first time, she questioned this, knowing she already had a school coach. This was the beginning of her healthy de-idealization of her father. She noted how he came to all her games but that it wasn't just because he loved her; as she told her mirror one day, it's "because he gets off on it! He likes having a daughter he can brag about."

Dale began to increasingly confide in her mother. Growing up, she looked to her father for self-definition, but it was becoming apparent that this was changing. She remarked to her mother, "How did I make him *this* important? It's like my whole life revolves around him, rather than me." This concerned her mother, who sought a psychological consultation about her daughter's anxiety. She knew Dale was very susceptible to her husband's dictates, as was she, and thought it reasonable for her daughter to question her motives in wanting a broader social life. This was huge progress for Dale's mother, as a parent who wanted to spare her daughter the excessive responsibilities she took for her father.

Dale wondered if her relationship with her narcissistic father was causing her social problems and debated with herself about the degree with which she should stay involved with him. She began to realize the relationship with her father was putting her broader interests outside the home at risk. She was self-doubting, due to her long history of providing her father with his narcissistic supplies. He still intruded upon her social life by frequently texting her at school and making her miss events. She limited interactions with her peers to placate and please him, actions she had taken earlier in her life. However, at this point in her development, appeasing her father and restricting peer interactions no longer brought her a sense of calm; to the contrary, they brought panic attacks.

After Dale talked about her panic attacks with her mother, who worried they would increase and were significant signs of an emotional disturbance, her mother found a psychological consult. She sought some intervention to prevent Dale's anxiety from escalating.

One specific panic attack was brought about by her father's intrusion into her activity as a writer for the school newspaper. When she wrote science articles, her father approved, but when she wanted to address political issues, he was disgruntled because this was not his interest. Dale was disappointed and anxious about wanting to please her father, as usual feeling a skewed responsibility to his needs. But she was gaining more self-confidence in asserting her wish to participate in other things, like this newspaper, that he didn't favor. She began to have the courage to contemplate how his primary interest seemed to be himself and his wishes and not her needs.

Due to her years of reverse parenting, there were many situations where her father could persuade her to do things she didn't want to do or persuade her not to do what she delighted in. But her father's control over her was fading because of her growing autonomy as a mid-adolescent. In a sense, all his efforts to make her a stellar athlete and student were now backfiring on him. She was adored by her teachers and friends for her leadership qualities and accomplishments, so much so that other adults were now entering her world and influencing her. She began to feel better about herself.

The narcissistic family model, or the parent-centered model, is about a parent system that mirrors only the parent's needs. It is about a child who only exists for this parent to the extent that she meets or refuses to meet his needs. The question now was if there was a possibility of productive change in the present family system.

The teacher who was the head of the school paper praised both Dale's science and political articles and encouraged her to strive to become editor of the paper. This teacher was pulling her out of her seclusion. Ironically, her father thought this teacher's praise of his daughter reflected well on him, but at the same time, he felt left out of this new sphere of adult influence on his daughter, and this injured his pride. Dale was still trying to get her father's approval, but now it was at the expense of feeling valued and respected by other adults whom she admired and her father envied. For the first time, Dale could find within herself conscious anger and resentment at her father for standing in her way. This was a significant change. To voice her blame on her father seemed contrary to her sense of self, yet to blame herself for wanting more than he could provide became a reasonable overriding issue that was new for Dale.

What brought about Dale's latest panic attack occurred when her father, without telling her, contacted the teacher who oversaw the school newspaper and demanded that Dale spend less time on political issues. Not understanding this father's disappointment in his stellar daughter, the teacher protested that the decision should be left up to her. No one, particularly no adult, had disagreed with his fathering before and given his daughter independence in problem-solving. His feelings were intensified when Dale found out from the teacher that her father had interfered. She felt surprised and humiliated that she wasn't included in this discussion.

Dale appreciated the teacher's recommendation that she make her own decision about what she wrote about. But she felt intensely anxious about this dispute between the two adults—both of whom were important to her. Her father called her selfish, which confused her. (In fact, his accusation that she was being self-centered was a projection of his attitude.) She had great difficulty tolerating this accusation, because she was developing her own value system, but at the same time, she still very much wanted her father's approval. Conflicted, she was filled with recurring self-doubt, wanting to have her father acknowledge the reality of her motivations. This confusion led to panic.

As we know, Dale was accustomed to seeking harmony with her father. At first, she did not want to take on the uncomfortable, distressing feelings of disagreeing with him. So, initially, she gave up her political writing. However, her peers questioned this decision, as they were picking up on her initiative and writing political articles themselves—following her lead.

Dale found herself torn between being compliant or, for the first time, rebellious. To defy her adored father was a huge step for her—even though it would be a sign of maturity. She sought her mother's advice. Her mother was deeply troubled by her daughter's quandary, fearing her narcissistic husband's response should she side with Dale, which indeed seemed to be the right approach. She was also still worried about her daughter's panic attacks and sought additional advice from the school psychologist. This was now the second time she had sought help outside of the home in child-rearing. At the suggestion of the school counselor, she introduced her husband to Parental Intelligence. This is a collaborative parenting approach that he viewed

as extraordinarily counterintuitive; he was a father who wanted dominance and control over his daughter's mind and activities.

However, Dale's mother felt pressure from the teacher at the
school, as well as the school counselor, who both wanted Dale to find
her own way. Dale's mother felt that she had to risk marital dissension
for Dale's benefit. She boldly took the step to share with her husband
that she'd had the psychological consult, in addition to meeting with
the school counselor. She indeed was feeling a bit more empowered
herself and believed her daughter should make her own judgments.
Because of concerns for her daughter, she confronted her husband:

"Dale is troubled, and it's because of your disagreement with her
about writing political articles for the school paper. You may not know
it, but your actions have led Dale to have a panic attack."

"I didn't know that."

"The school psychologist has taught me about an approach called
Parental Intelligence."

Dale's father was astounded that his wife had sought help outside
the family and felt hurt and injured for not being consulted. But he
at first half-heartedly listened, sensing it was in his best interest as a
father and husband—especially since his daughter had had a panic
attack.

"I'd like us to try this approach," his wife said. "I found it very
interesting. There are five steps to approaching a problem."

"Is this anything like the problem-solving techniques I've seen at
our lab?"

"Maybe," his wife replied. "There is a step called *problem-solving*,
but it's the last step. There are others before that. The first step is *stepping back*, where we don't make any decisions but just consider what's
occurring."

"What does that mean?"

"We pause nonjudgmentally," his wife continued, "to understand
the situation and understand what's happening without reacting."

"Okay," Dale's father replied.

"For example, if we know Dale has had a panic attack, we don't
immediately jump into action. We stop, wait, and . . . well, just let the
information sink in."

"I would want to do something."

"I understand, but it's better if we wait. Next, we do something more difficult called *self-reflecting*, where we look inside ourselves at our own feelings about the problem."

As I will discuss in a later chapter, Dale's father is an example of the narcissistic man who, given the appropriate supports—in this case, the concept laid out in Parental Intelligence—is able to make important changes in the way he approaches the world. At first, he was taken aback by his wife's initiative. Yet, deeply inside himself, he also applauded it. He wanted to be proud of his wife, as a reflection of himself as a good husband. So, he tentatively said he'd try the Parental Intelligence approach. Stepping back was easy. They both saw the new rebellious attitude Dale had as her way of trying to please all adults, as well as have her own points of view.

During the self-reflecting step, he most reluctantly admitted that he was deeply injured because Dale was swayed by the teacher in school, rather than just by him. But he was also able to admit that this teacher's confidence in Dale reflected well on them as parents.

Having had so many years living with her narcissistic husband, Dale's mother knew that affirming all the sacrifices and care her husband had given Dale over the years would appeal to his pride—even selfishness. She did this, which in time led to his becoming more resilient. One of the first signs of his change was when he no longer saw his daughter's wish to write the kinds of articles she wanted as a personal affront. This was a huge step for such a self-centered man. Dale's mother was elated that her husband was loosening some of his control. They moved on to the third step of Parental Intelligence: *understanding your child's mind*.

This was another large leap for this dad, who only considered what was on *his* mind most of the time. He had to bear the responsibility that he had molded his daughter in his own fashion without recognizing her inner growth. But he had noticed at work that other scientists gave him good ideas, and he was becoming open to working with them; after all, it might lead to a promotion for him. Though egotistically and inconsiderately motivated, he pondered whether he should give Dale the same respect, thinking how it might aggrandize him as the father of a stellar daughter. The following discussion took place at dinner that night:

Dad: "Dale, your mother and teacher at school want you to decide for yourself the kinds of articles you want to write for the school newspaper. I know I've been tough about my preferences, but your mother has convinced me to consider your point of view. How do you feel about all this?"

Dale: "I'm shaken, Dad, that you want my point of view. It makes me very nervous, because I don't want to displease you. But honestly, I've found that writing about political issues has opened up a new world for me; my friends and my teacher seem to think I write very well on this topic. I do have you to thank for helping me be a good writer. [This comment was genuine on Dale's part. It recognized what a narcissist can offer his child but was also a way to give him the narcissistic supply of admiration that he coveted.] All the scientific research you've exposed me to has led me to learn how to be a good, organized writer." [Dale was taking responsibility for her accomplishments, a new attitude that didn't just reflect her father's judgment.]

Dad: "Thank you for recognizing that I have helped you, even though I'm disappointed you don't favor the science writing, which is superior to political issues."

Dale: "Actually some of the scientific research that you do has a political ring to it. There is controversy that you have shared with me about how genetic research gains the greater endowments from the corporations, who I think are politically influenced. Don't you think that's true?" [Again, she drew on his need for narcissistic admiration; she loved her father and did believe he was trying hard to be a good parent.]

Dad: "That is interesting to contemplate. Would you like to write an article about that? It would please us both."

Dale was feeling a new sense of mastery and control. It was the first time she really looked at the way her father had reared her. She was seeing the reality of her upbringing.

> Dale: "Sure. That's exciting. Can I interview some of the people that you work with to find out differing points of view?"

> Dad: "Yes. I can arrange that." [By making the arrangements, he resumed some feeling of control. Plus, he also knew that having his colleagues see what a good science writer his daughter was becoming would be a feather in both their caps.]

Dale's mother was incredibly gratified by this discussion. It seemed that her husband was not as controlling as she had expected. She didn't really expect him to follow the next step of Parental Intelligence: *understanding your child's development*, but she knew that, in effect, that's what was going on. Dale was being encouraged to think for herself—with her father's approval. This was a substantial adolescent challenge and a major change for both father and daughter.

The last step was *problem-solving*, which, in effect, had already taken place. Dale was going to present their idea to her teacher the next day.

As the compliant child who had always been with her narcissistic father (Brown 2008), Dale had constantly monitored her father's signs of distress and unmet needs. But she was able to include his interests in her problem-solving, so she didn't feel the guilt she would normally feel when he might be disappointed or disagree with her. Whereas she had formerly been fearful of disagreements with him or any form of conflict, she seemed to carefully include him in her reasoning, rather than feel or act rebellious. She didn't withdraw from the conflict as she normally would. She was facing that she did not have a perfect father, but he was a human being who was capable of change within his parameters of self-centeredness. In maintaining the idealized version of her father when she was younger, she was facing both the de-idealization process of her father and the shift in her own sources of narcissistic satisfaction that are so necessary to healthy adolescent development.

This was a turning point in Dale's adolescent life. Her father's beginning attunement to her needs built her self-esteem. Her father's parental message was a powerful influence on them both going forward. They learned to have discussions from different points of view that loosened his tight control over her mind. He saw, with self-reflecting, that he could indeed survive without feeling humiliated by stretching his capacity to compromise. He didn't feel abandoned by his daughter but felt that she prized his opinions, fostering his narcissistic needs while expanding his capacity to see beyond them. Dale, for her part, realized she didn't need to rebel against her father, but they could have dialogues she never expected.

Dale's mother was deeply relieved that her husband loosened his control over their daughter—at least this time. It gave her hope for the future; hopefully, Dale could take care of her own needs without sacrificing her father's longings to be affirmed for his desires at all times. He was capable of compromise, a most important shift for a narcissistic man. Deep down, she believed that it was his love for their daughter that allowed him to tackle the steps of Parental Intelligence (Hollman 2015).

Dale now had a social network in school as a safe space to work, finding herself less isolated by her father. She became much less reclusive and secluded. She was able to supply herself with new dreams, new goals, new friendships, a growing relationship with her mother, and space and time for healing. This was deeply significant for this teenager. Also significant was that the threat of the rupture of this father-daughter narcissistic relationship did not cause instability or fragmentation in the father; he was more resilient than might have been anticipated.

As a younger child, Dale didn't know her own feelings, because her father never asked for them. He was focused on his own feelings and needs, and so was she. With this newfound recognition, she began to bloom, as other adults in her environment valued her views and recognized that her role in life was not only to serve others. This did not require blame or judgment, confrontation or forgiveness. It simply was a recognition of how she could relearn her role in her family to make her life more satisfying.

While she had been molded by her past experiences, she no longer needed to be defined by them. She was now able to think about what *she* observed, thought, and felt. She was able to begin to develop a mature ego ideal that included her own aspirations and ambitions. This permitted her to observe her parents more realistically, which liberated her energy and attention so that she could be more involved with herself and her peers.

It would be helpful at this juncture to refer back to the conclusion of chapter two, where the five characteristics of healthy self-love are enumerated. They apply well to Dale's needs that her father was able to accept as they fostered her adolescent development. In raising *healthy* narcissistic children, it is important to model this healthy self-love.

CHAPTER NINE

Females and Their Narcissistic Men

How Spouses of Narcissists Can Live Happy, Healthy Lives

We have met three couples, all with pathologically narcissistic men and codependent women, and one pathologically narcissistic father with a teenage daughter. In this chapter, we look to further understand these females who eventually formed healthier senses of self. Each was seriously at risk emotionally, and each needed a connection with someone who could offer unconditional acceptance, affirmation, and validation in order to feel restored.

We need to ask some questions. What conditions contributed to their codependency that made them vulnerable to narcissistic men?

What are the factors involved in the codependent/narcissistic dynamic? And finally, how does the codependent female begin to bring about the kinds of changes that allow her to be more independent, yet at the same time preserve her intimate relationship—if possible and wanted?

Conditions Contributing to Codependency that Make Women Vulnerable to Narcissistic Men

We have seen how the codependent (without outside help) will respond to the less healthy partner with a lack of awareness and respect for the inherent rights and needs of herself. According to Payson (2017),

> the codependent suffers from a mental paradigm that places herself as less important than others. Her painful feelings, usually interpreted as reinforcement that she is inadequate and unlovable, keep her stuck in confusion and self-doubt. . . . In order to regain her wholeness, the codependent must recognize her emotional depletion and seek therapeutic assistance. (75)

Regardless of their insecurities, the codependent women had greater accessibility to their own thoughts and feelings than the narcissistic men in these cases. Laura and Ava were more capable of self-reflection and self-examination, with feedback from me as their therapist. They could empathize with their own feelings and those of others. Thus, their capacity to regulate their feelings and impulses considerably improved with treatment and as they worked on their relationships with their narcissistic husbands. However, their feelings of pain and low self-esteem surrounding their experiences would often return, bringing attendant anxiety and depressed moods.

Factors Involved in the Codependent/Narcissistic Dynamic

This brings us to the common characteristics of the codependent: unreasonable neurotic guilt and the partial suppression of justifiable anger. Laura, for example, became burdened by guilt because she couldn't remedy the pathology of her loved one—even though *he* hurt *her* immensely with his betrayal. She would often prioritize his needs at the cost of herself.

Thus, the codependent wife often suppresses selective feelings related to her personal autonomy and aspirations. Her naturally healthy desires for accomplishment and independence conflict with her deep feelings of insecurity and wishes for connection and approval. These dependency needs can make it difficult for the codependent to find the courage to venture beyond her comfort zone and risk the fulfillment of her goals and ambitions. This was the case for Laura, who got scattered and disorganized and then procrastinated when reaching for her own aspirations.

Thus, Laura fell into interpersonal patterns of behavior that satisfied her husband's needs, rather than her own, further depleting her sense of self (Payson 2017). In other words, she was predisposed to be other-directed, responding to the needs of others before herself. This corresponded to her upbringing, where she inhibited her own needs in order to affirm her self-absorbed parents. This pattern continued in her married life until she was supported by my therapy; she then began to seek satisfaction from her abilities and design her own ambitions. Divorce was ultimately the action that set her on her own path to independent functioning and self-confidence.

> Therefore, the child with codependent neurotic wounding is selectively given narcissistic supplies primarily when she performs other-directed caretaking behaviors and she begins to internalize that the needs of others take priority over her own. This is often the beginning of the emotional and

developmental wounding that leads to the eventual issues we see in the codependent neurotic individual. (Payson 2017, 67)

This was much more the case for Laura than Ava, however, who was most accomplished as a pediatrician. However, even Ava needed to learn in psychotherapy how far to extend herself as a doctor with her patients—for whom she was too much a caregiver, not respecting their needed autonomy and her own boundaries. (She would give them her cell number, text them unnecessarily, and often attend their functions as if she were more of a friend.)

Wade's narcissistic tendency to become obsessed with what Ava was doing, a tendency to control reality to shore up his grandiose self, matched her codependent need to be looked after—even though she complained it was too intrusive and overwhelming. This dynamic backfired frequently, however, when she experienced his actions as being self-absorbed and not attuned to her needs. She would abruptly leave the house in a rage, not telling him where she was going to collect herself and refind her equilibrium.

Ava also needed to gain more self-respect by enjoying and receiving pleasures from hobbies. As her jewelry-making became lucrative, it was devalued by her husband, as well as her children (in identification with their father's dismissals of Ava's creative pursuits).

Ava, unlike Laura, possessed more healthy self-assertion in the pursuit of her ambitions. Yet she remained passive and avoidant at first, regarding her needs and rights within her intimate relationship. She came to that later—with the help of treatment. In that sense, Ava was more high functioning as a codependent woman than the other two wives in this study.

If the woman's spouse also attends treatment, this can help them with their relationship. Thus, when Wade began individual treatment with me, he began to reckon with Ava's distress and gain some capacity for self-reflection. He was able to connect more with her true feelings. While at first he had demonstrated a powerful possessive need to dominate her every move, choice, and thought, he began to recognize the nature of her painful feelings. This transformation was due to her descriptions of her upbringing to me in her therapy that she then shared with her husband. He then became aware of her profound need to heal from within. Thus, when she became more open about her past, he showed compassion (with my therapeutic support) that made him more vulnerable. He began to discover more of Ava's whole and authentic self—one rooted in the unconditional worthiness of her being (Payson 2017).

Rio did not reveal too much about his Swedish wife, a younger woman named Eli, because that took away from his self-centered focus. But apparently she was an immigrant from a poor family and had shaky self-esteem. She was too focused on her appearance, despite his perception of her supposed beauty. We may assume that her outward appearance and inner presence weren't validated as she was growing up. Coming alone to America left her on shaky ground, as there was no one to consistently confirm her worthiness. She experienced herself as deficient and thus attached herself to Rio in order to feel more competent. Because Rio was successful and relatively supportive of Eli's work life, her dependency improved her self-esteem. However, she must have felt his ambivalence toward her achievements. She tried to dress impeccably to satisfy Rio's need for a trophy wife but was unable to consistently elicit his affirmation, attention, and approval. Although conditional, the affirmations that he did give her were preferable to the pain of being ignored or criticized, which would be humiliating for this immigrant. She did not feel a solid sense of self like the American women whom she idealized. This focus on her external appearance suggests that for some reason she became increasingly preoccupied with her external self because her internal self was not grounded. For example, Rio was also preoccupied with externals, so he reinforced her desires for plastic surgery. He viewed these desires as needs that should be met because "That's how the world is." Thus, their codependent/narcissistic duo was constantly being reinforced by the other. They didn't understand worthiness for just *being*.

However, for Laura, Ava, and younger Dale, intense inner conflict propelled and enabled them to take a deeper look at themselves and their lives. They began to recognize and reevaluate their distorted perceptions and discover their healthier sense of self.

As Dale entered adolescence, her natural healthy development triggered her shift from being the parentified child. With the support of her mother and school teachers, she detached herself from her father's narcissistic hold and became more able to assert her needs in a healthy way. Out of his love for her, Dale's father let go of his tight hold on Dale's behavior and became able to support her healthy development—a major shift for him.

> Over time, the codependent's defenses, initially designed to protect against abandonment, lead to self-abandonment as her interpersonal relationships erode her vitality and emotional resilience. . . . Fortunately, because codependent neurotic issues are ego dystonic [conflictual], and because she has the skills of self-reflection and empathy, this individual is far more likely to engage and remain committed to the therapeutic challenge of reclaiming her wholeness. (Payson 2017, 78)

Bringing About Change as a Codependent Woman

Let's now look into the various ways that a codependent woman can be happy, if possible, in a narcissistic relationship. Each woman needs to decide for herself (with professional support) what she hopes to gain from her significant relationship. Each woman in this book had a different point of view, depending on her history and personal goals and ambitions.

Reclaiming the Self

Recovering from codependent neurosis begins with giving up the beliefs of unworthiness and inadequacy. This requires learning to set boundaries and saying no to those who do not support the woman's or girl's well-being. Each woman and adolescent begins to become aware of the challenges of a healthy sense of self with the inner support of a compassionate witness from a personal network of support (Dale's mother and teachers) or a therapist (myself) who listens nonjudgmentally.

It is important for the codependent woman or adolescent not to be judgmental of herself, subtly sabotaging her attempts at assertion, sound decision-making, and the right to hold others accountable for their actions in order to preserve one's own dignity and respect *without exception*. This comes with the acceptance that there are enough rights and positive attention for each person in a relationship. It's important to keep in mind the narcissistic/codependent relationship where there is an asymmetrical exchange of narcissistic supplies, devaluing messages, and boundary violations. It is essential for the codependent women and adolescent to be cautious about eroding *their* self-esteem while bolstering the grandiose self of the narcissist.

It is too easy for the codependent to acquiesce to the narcissist. This occurs because she experiences a confused and self-doubting position often defensively spoken of by the codependent as "It takes two" to cause the problems—when in fact the two sides are not in any way equivalent. (Laura often asked what she did wrong to lead to her husband's infidelities, saying she wasn't perfect either. But she came to see that her actions were certainly not equivalent to his disloyalty.)

The narcissist's contribution to the disturbed relationship needs to be accurately assessed. Clues to this circumstance for the codependent are feelings of anxiety, confusion, destabilization, and disorientation. When feeling such uneasiness, it's important to sense something is wrong in the codependent's reality testing, rather than continue to behave as if everything is normal when it is not. Doing so could consequently undermine the woman's sense of confidence.

Three of the four codependents in this book began to make healthy strides by becoming involved in an expressive activity that had nothing to do with their relationship to a narcissistic man.

Laura became an accomplished designer of collages. Her adept self-expression with collage-making was a rather hidden talent that her husband disparaged as frivolous—even though she was quite adept at it. Using this medium, she was able to express her conflicts pictorially. Eventually, to her credit and developmental growth, she successfully showed her artwork in local galleries.

In Ava's case, her artful jewelry-making led not only to praise for her work but significant monetary gains. Substantial money made through her art not only gave her confidence as a jewelry-maker but as a person, as well. Because it occurred to her during her time in therapy, she related it to her progress toward a healthy life.

Dale, too, began to recognize her writing ability when it was affirmed by her teachers and peers. Her mother's support further enhanced her capacity to recognize her talents and ambitions.

Thus, both women and the adolescent girl found creative artistic means to express themselves and eventually solidify their self-esteem.

The longer the codependency/narcissistic dynamic has gone on, the harder it may be to change it. When the codependent feels depleted, it becomes very difficult to make independent decisions and become the center of one's own initiative. It is easy to destabilize and disorient a codependent person and lead them to their vulnerable tendency to self-doubt and feelings of uncertainty. This is epitomized by the narcissist's refusal to communicate directly, which was the case with Clive and Laura over his years of infidelity, as he drew on her vulnerable, sympathetic nature. This was also epitomized by Wade and Dale's father's conflicted beliefs in Ava and Dale's accomplishments, which added to their self-doubts.

It's essential for the codependent to ask herself, "What does he do to make me feel the most vulnerable?" After answering this, she can identify signals to her sensitivities that make her feel defenseless and helpless. It is imperative for the codependent who is trying to assert herself to know when she is being sidetracked by the narcissist's interruptions or distractions by taking time out when in doubt.

It's equally important for the codependent who is trying to create a change in the dynamic with the narcissistic individual (her husband or father) to not react impulsively. If her assertion is sidetracked by the narcissist too persistently, it becomes necessary to discontinue the conversation, get a grip on herself, and not be derailed.

Laura allowed Clive to retreat to another part of the house when she was derailed from her own expressions of ideas. He would ignore her questions and go to what he designated as *his* room. This gave her time to reflect. Eventually, when she came to respect her own needs more fully, she realized that divorce was inevitable in order for her to sustain her own identity.

As you may recall, Ava would leave the house when Wade was persistent in over-talking to her and she felt her voice wasn't heard. Wade interrupted her attempts to declare her feelings and set off her rage reaction, which she controlled by physically disengaging from the home to regain her emotional equilibrium. What helped her eventually was directly defining the behavior change she needed from him in order to prevent his lengthy digressive explanations that were conversation stoppers. This worked even when he was too self-centered to fully understand how he was disturbing her, because he indeed loved her and didn't want her to dismiss him. She learned to clearly and succinctly specify the behavior change she wanted, such as, "When we go on outings, I want time to relax and be by myself if necessary, while you pursue all the sights." This eventually worked very effectively, and they began to enjoy their travels together. Thus, Ava specified particular behavioral changes that couldn't be refuted easily or couldn't become defocused through persistent conversation on Clive's part, thus derailing her request. In effect, as Ava's self-esteem improved, she changed herself, which resulted in her husband's change.

Gaining time alone to self-reflect was effective in the lives of Laura, Ava, and Dale because "mutuality, reciprocity, and authentic exchange represent the core values that so elude the narcissist" (Payson 2017, 130).

This does not mean Laura, Ava, or Dale held more personal responsibility for their dynamics than their husbands or father, but that they had empowered themselves to withstand the men's narcissistic strategies.

Wade had no choice but to accept Laura's line of thought, because she decided to divorce him. Clive had to eventually give up (at least partially) his belief that Ava was the "crazy one." Dale's father's change came about after he read, understood, and began acting on the ideas outlined in the collaborative Parental Intelligence approach.

Let me end this chapter by addressing the issue of a false equivalency: the situation where the narcissist requires most of the "sustenance" in a relationship while arguing that everything is equal. In three of the four cases discussed, the codependents make major changes in their lives by confronting this issue. Wade, Clive, and Dale's father needed to take responsibility for their parts in their problems, even though they held firmly and defensively to the belief that they were not causative agents of disagreements. They lacked the ability to reflect upon their relationships with an objective understanding of their impact on their wives and daughter's sense of self. The ultimate wounding experienced by Laura, Ava, and Dale did not only occur from the injuries themselves (such as lack of empathy) but from the lack of support to deal authentically with their feelings about these injuries (Payson 2017). This became my role as their therapist and Dale's mother's role as a more active parent.

Action Items for Spouses of Narcissistic Men

1. Seek support from a mental health professional who can help you view your self-image realistically.
2. Ask yourself, "What made me vulnerable to this narcissistic man?"
3. Clarify your own goals and ambitions.
4. Question your own ability to feel and be independent in life.
5. Become more introspective, reflecting on your own realistic strengths and weaknesses.
6. Challenge yourself to build new interests and learning opportunities.
7. Reflect upon your need to feel dependent on a grandiose man.
8. Allow yourself a range of feelings, including anger toward the narcissistic man in your life.
9. Develop your own voice and express it.
10. Become the center of your own initiative.
11. Clarify your values and let them be your compass in finding a direction.

CHAPTER TEN

Can the Narcissist Change?

First, we need to review once again who the narcissist is—keeping in mind that, while there are similarities, each narcissist is different in his capacity for change.

When mythological Narcissus fell in love, it was with his own image—an illusion. The person who tries to establish love with a narcissist may only do so if she is willing to reflect the narcissist's own views. It means that the woman reflects the narcissist's ideas and repeats his voice or opinion. When she can no longer do this, the narcissist is vulnerable, because he only subconsciously knows the self-image he has built. He is obsessed with illusions of power, brilliance, beauty, and ideal love but unwilling (or unable) to recognize or identify with the feelings or needs of others. The narcissist feels superior to others and wishes to control and dominate; he craves attention and resents it when others are in the spotlight.

Feeling they are special, narcissists want to associate with others whom they believe are as unique and special as they are. In the extreme, they have unreasonable expectations of others—without feeling gratitude. They feel entitled and are resentful when others have what they want. Some narcissists assume that other people are envious of them. The crux of the matter is that narcissists mostly deceive people into believing them to be charming and outstanding models of society, only showing their true selves to those most devoted to them. Newfound fame or wealth can increase narcissism.

Even though some narcissists may not publicly fly into rages and may appear humble and kind, they can be as ruthless. Both the overt and covert narcissists have feelings of insecurity and resort to what is needed in order to get affirmation and praise. The overt narcissist may use intimidation, while the covert will use more passive-aggressive methods. Little or no guilt is felt in taking from others or putting others down to get what they want. When narcissists give, it is to get something in return. The men in this book—young university student Carver, personal injury lawyer Wade, neurosurgeon Clive, commodity trader Rio, and neuroscientist Dale's father—all had overt qualities of success and dominance and covert qualities of vulnerability and inferiority that they persistently sought to compensate for and did so rather brilliantly.

Recall that narcissistic traits are present in everyone and are responsible for positive qualities, such as self-esteem, confidence, ambition, creativity, and general well-being. It is a healthy self-love that enables a person to love others well. The narcissistic men mentioned here could not do this. They appeared exciting and likeable—valued for their confidence, leadership, and innovation—but when their traits became excessive, imagined, and pathological, the failures in their relationships became evident.

For these men, their careers, spouses, coworkers, children, and even strangers fulfilled their narcissistic supplies until they experienced rejection or instability in their work or daily life.

Each of these men were very image-conscious, wanting to appear normal, stable, influential, and dominating. In fact, they were successful for the most part, which misled others into believing they were stable. However, whenever the narcissistic supply was blocked, they felt slighted and injured. Overt or covert rage was their reaction to the blocking of their supplies. For all these men (except Rio and Carver), the rage was usually covert and passive-aggressive. Lawyer Wade would shut out his spouse and use silent treatment and dismissal to conceal his rage. Neurosurgeon Clive would putter about endlessly in his home, never relaxing but concealing his rage in hyperactivity and confusion when his needs were questioned by his spouse. Dale's father used silent treatment toward his daughter when he didn't feel she was responding to his needs. Conversely, commodity trader Rio revealed his rage when he didn't feel understood or reacted to in the way he prescribed in therapy. His onetime success when he made his millions did not erase his vulnerability, because he could not continue to make a larger fortune or feel satisfied with friends or his wife. Carver expressed his rage openly at his parents and siblings, feeling this self-expression was his due.

None of these men or young Carver felt any consistent remorse for those they hurt. Ultimately, their own personal gain was what mattered, despite any publicly portrayed illusions to the contrary. So, how could they change?

All five men changed, at least in part. Let's take a look:

Carver

Teenagers can typically be self-centered, but they eventually grow out of it. Narcissistic, self-absorbed teenagers, however, exhibit the same traits as the adult narcissist—but those traits may be misconstrued as a stage in their development. Not so for Carver, who openly admitted his fears of being unlikeable, his self-loathing, and his deep sense of inferiority. In his household, however, he was cruel, sadistic, and ruthlessly critical of his siblings, whom he envied for his mother's attention. These actions temporarily empowered him but couldn't mask his vulnerability.

As a middle-adolescent, Carver saw himself in some ways as superior and more talented, and he was filled with self-praise. He became angry and resentful, even aggressive, when this image of himself was questioned socially. He lacked empathy and believed the world owed him, even claiming it was his wealthy birthright to receive the accolades he prized and to do anything he liked—even if it was morally, emotionally, or physically damaging to others. He couldn't seem to get along with most of his peers, whom he wanted to dominate; he had difficulty establishing healthy relationships. Underneath his bravado was prolonged sadness attended by periodic lethargy, irritability, anger, tearfulness, mood swings, and withdrawal from others, all often accompanied by irregular eating-and-sleeping habits. He was prone to depressive episodes, bouts of rage, panic attacks, and general instability.

When he was an older adolescent, psychotherapy helped appreciably to stabilize his moods, set him on a positive academic path, and recover from social rejections more quickly. Now, when windows closed, he sought others to open. He joined new clubs with his peers and took on leadership roles with responsibility. His grades were excellent, and he interviewed well for various positions on campus. Consequently, he became less likely to believe he could get away with taking advantage of others, though he persistently maneuvered his parents to give him what he wanted in the way of possessions and special outings. Of particular importance in his changing was when he began to recognize that his association with high-status peers did not increase his value as a person. That represented real growth. He had a long journey ahead but began to ask the right questions. Did he expect too much? Could he have different perspectives? Should he feel guilty for the way he treated his siblings? Was he selfish? What were *realistic* steps he needed to take to meet his aspirations? These questions were major changes in his path to improved mental health.

Laura and Wade

Vulnerability can be seen in actions that betray its existence. For example, from the beginning as a young student, Laura was lavished with attention and praise from Wade, who seemed totally enamored with her at first and intermittently during their marriage. Eventually, he began to say that Laura held him back from his persistent need to go on outings to concerts, plays, travel, and expensive dinners, as she wanted to remain unhurried at home. He made her feel rejected and ashamed, but she couldn't understand what was happening; thirty-five years went by without her knowing that Wade was deceiving her with infidelities. In daily conversation, he accused others of being liars, narcissists, misogynists, and cheaters—actually projecting his own characteristics onto those around him. But even after decades of marriage, when she learned of his betrayal, he bombarded her with presents, texts, flowers, and phone calls. She wanted to appreciate these efforts but felt herself getting colder and colder toward him, not being able to withstand his touch.

She no longer favored his smooth, charming manner that had attracted her in the beginning. He gave her the silent treatment when she questioned his motives and actions, a classic passive-aggressive tactic. It was his way of putting her down without using words, assuming control. Later, he treated her as though nothing had happened, leaving her mystified and clueless. She remained this way until she was in treatment, and then she began to find herself living with a very vulnerable and unstable man. He envied her relationships with their children and her ordinary friends. She now observed his maneuvers publicly as trying to seek adoration from others who were often exemplary or famous in their lines of work. His vulnerability became more obvious, and she sympathized but from a more remote position than before.

As he would apologize for his cheating and say he felt ashamed, Wade expected things to go back to normal. He may or may not have sounded sincere in showing his remorse, but what was strange was his expectation that things could get back to their normal way of living. She, too, tried to live a normal life, but when she did so she felt like the liar that he was. It made her disoriented, disorganized, and unstable. Only when she confronted and examined herself for fearing success on her own could she see a clearer future for herself—as an independent woman.

In time, Laura asked for a divorce because she saw that Wade was unable to give the kind of substantial change she needed. As my patient, she expressed hope that Wade would make the positive changes she knew he had to make, but she could no longer tolerate remaining in the relationship. Although Wade entered therapy for a while, he quit—showing himself to be an example of the narcissist who has trouble openly communicating and accepting the limits of the therapy setting, where he couldn't dominate and control the situation. Later, he sought another therapist and remained in treatment. After reconciling with Laura's independent actions—her accomplishments such as exhibiting her collage-making; her career path; and ultimately, her choice to divorce—hopefully, Wade will be able to question his shortcomings and confusions, at least in their relationship.

Ava and Clive

Ava learned that subtle manipulation was not always easy to detect, but when Clive dismissed her excellent career, her profitable hobby, and her sanity, she knew she was up against a difficult narcissist. When she lost her self-confidence and assertiveness and felt unsure about herself, finding it difficult to have her opinions heard, she began to feel mistreated. She felt sad, depressed, anxious, and uneasy, finding it hard to enjoy the things she liked to do because they were demeaned by him. Her needs were treated as unfounded and her feelings were dismissed. She was viewed as crazy by this self-empowered successful man.

However, when she questioned his motives and actions, his vulnerability came to the fore. When she independently took actions to leave the house on her own, he felt shocked and slighted beyond belief. He found it absolutely incredible that she would leave him for a weekend, for example, to explore her own inner needs, build her self-esteem, and relax on her own. He had trouble understanding her wishes to not always follow his overactive, excessive needs to persistently go to random concerts, plays, and museums, and he found himself regarding his situation as unfair. He became anxious and unsettled, no longer enjoying all the things he was used to doing. Ava questioned his parenting, his medical practices, and his verbose over-talking in company, and as a result he was beside himself with vulnerability—all of which led him to agree to marital therapy with me. However, when it was pointed out that he was so dominating in the joint sessions (Ava actually walked out once), he eventually agreed to go into his own separate therapy with me, where he gradually began to make some substantive changes for the better.

What was striking about Clive was his lack of awareness surrounding when he was being so unmistakably inattentive. His self-observing function was not in operation, leaving Ava feeling like she was nonexistent to him at certain moments. Ava's manifestations of her aggression toward Clive were revealed in her withdrawals when she was furious. She withdrew both to protect others from her wrath and as an action that expressed her anger safely. However, she became angry when he detached from her, with his preoccupation with himself or with his dismissal of her feelings and views.

He had the mistaken sense of doing all the giving but not receiving love and sexual gratification in return. He began to realize this was not true during our therapy; this awakened him to his plight in their failing relationship. He had to question his kindness and good intentions and ascertain if he took advantage of Ava's needs. He had to face the fact that he was not a good listener. Although he tried to convince himself that he was genuinely interested in her views, he was openly critical of her disagreement with his needs for status, his over-involvement with their teenagers and college students' academic studies, and eventually, all his networking to ensure his kids some job success.

Only when the young adult children complained to their mother that their father lacked boundaries and was interfering in their lives did Clive gain some acceptance of his inappropriate actions—if not real awareness of his motivations. He didn't feel he was wrong; however, he accepted their displeasure as something he had to go along with—to his chagrin. He felt that without him, his children would not succeed. This had some questionable merit because of his initial neglect of their early schoolwork due to his self-absorption in his own career. As they became adolescents, they did not develop academic independence, so he filled in where they lacked in their school and college work assignments, trying to teach them how to organize their assignments. As an expression of his narcissism, he often ended up doing their work for them; he could not, would not tolerate their failure, because it would be a black mark against him.

He also tried triangulation with his children, pitting especially one daughter against his wife. But this daughter eventually put a stop to this when Clive disrupted her work life with all his calls and texts. He tried to pass the blame on to his wife to make her feel guilty, but his daughter was beyond this maneuver, so he could no longer trespass on his daughter at her work. He remained convinced that he had done no wrong but behaviorally changed to keep Ava's loyalty in their marriage. This worked. When I helped Wade see that the clearer boundaries his wife was setting would help, their marriage improved. She set new rules for his narcissistic behaviors (such as including her in decision-making when they traveled), and while he didn't understand, he followed; he did care about her and her supply of his narcissistic needs.

As she focused on rebuilding her self-esteem, meeting her own needs, and pursuing her interests, Ava realized that her value as a person did not depend on her narcissistic husband. Since he wanted a good relationship with her and their children, she learned to appeal to his actual self-centeredness by telling him what to do to get what she wanted. She had no desire to leave him, wanting to sustain the structure of their basically good life. She just went about doing what she wanted, regardless of his views, which even included redesigning their home to meet her needs for the future. Her experience made her wiser and stronger, and in time they had a healthier relationship where she could love herself.

Wade changed his behaviors (to some degree) because he loved his wife and children and saw the effects his actions had on them, according to his wife. He accepted Ava's mandatory time to herself, acknowledged her jewelry-making, recognized his children's need for more independence from him to some extent, and evolved into a man somewhat more aware. He had to learn to become capable of listening to others' views if he wanted good relationships.

Rio

Rio had the greatest difficulty changing in most respects, because he was limited in his ability to hear other perspectives and points of view about relationships. In his therapy, he mostly wanted his narcissistic thinking to be mirrored and understood. He resisted carefully considering that his need to change from his monogamous relationship with Eli to his imagined, empowering, wished-for relationships with many women could lead to loneliness and a lack of fulfillment. Eli made few demands upon him, so he was dependent ultimately on his own unsteady morality to make decisions. He eventually realized that, as his therapist, I could not make a specific decision for him to carry out his choice of such a future life. He had to be the decision-maker—especially concerning a future lifestyle of frequently entering casual sexual relationships with women. The only clearly evident change Rio made that was that he questioned his once-solid beliefs: that everyone believed in his worldview and that there always had to be an advantage in exchange for something, a philosophy of exploitation that in his mind determined all relationships with others. The beginning awareness that relationships could bring reciprocity and mutuality offered him a new way to figure out his choices for future relationships.

Dale and Her Father

Dale's father showed the most capacity for change. When his daughter's adolescent development led her to want to detach from her parentified role, he was able to listen to his wife's advice and engage in a new approach to parenting. This was indeed to his credit and resilience as a narcissistic father. His love for his wife and daughter took precedence over his grandiosity and needs for affirmation from them. His pathological narcissism was not as entrenched as the other men; he saw that Dale's aspirations as a writer were worthwhile and accepted her views of what to write about. This came about from the influence of his wife, the effects of listening to his daughter's points of view, and the results of collaborative family discussions that were modeled around the ideas of Parental Intelligence.

Some Thoughts on the Effects of Trauma on the Brain

In conclusion, the vulnerability of these men led to their spouses and children becoming aware of their own invisible battle wounds that had deeply affected the quality of their lives, happiness, security, and confidence. It is thought that there are effects of such trauma on the brain (Arabi 2017). Arabi explains that the amygdala in the brain (the part that processes emotions) becomes hyperactive when someone is traumatized, while the medial prefrontal cortex and hippocampus (the parts that deal with learning, memory, and decision-making) are dampened in the face of trauma. Toxic self-blame prevents the injured from forgiving themselves and causes them to judge themselves harshly, hindering the healing pathway significantly. This was the case for the women in this study.

It's important to realize the effects that this relationship trauma has on the brain in order to better understand why it takes the codependents of the narcissists so much time to understand themselves and the way the trauma has affected them. Many sufferers of narcissistic behaviors

> feel like they are in a "fog" of confusion, constantly distracted, unable to focus and make decisions without second-guessing themselves constantly. . . . The parts of the brain that deal with planning, cognition, learning, and decision-making become disconnected with the emotional parts of our brain—they can cease to talk to each other when an individual becomes traumatized. Professional support, validation and tailored resources are needed for the survivor to begin the dialogue between the trauma and the self. (Arabi 2017, 329)

We have seen how these narcissistic men were masters at playing mind games and covert manipulation. Survivors (codependents) are then subjected to a battle within their own minds about whether the reality they experience is truly exploitation, because the narcissist presents a false image of grandeur to the world, which supports their denial. This is a type of cognitive dissonance that encourages blaming. Once narcissists have their partners sufficiently controlled, they begin to devalue them and mistreat them (Arabi 2017). "Self-blame is often a symptom of the trauma experienced, but it can evolve into self-forgiveness and self-compassion on the healing journey" (245)—as we saw when most of the codependents reclaimed themselves.

Thus, with an extraordinary amount of introspection and support, many narcissists can make some changes that affect their relationships. However, this is a daunting therapeutic task for most, and a positive outlook for the narcissist to change significantly over the long haul remains in question. Certainly, however, specific changes occur and should be recognized as these men struggle with the impact of their past lives on their present situations.

CHAPTER ELEVEN

How Are Narcissism and Normal Love Different?

The rapprochement crisis happens when a child reacts to the loss of his omnipotence and that of his parents' undivided tie to him. The resolution of this crisis has major significance for later development—especially the child's capacity to deal with conflict.

In considering the examples of narcissistic men in this study, the reader will question the difference between a narcissistic relationship and one that could be considered normal. In this chapter, I want to outline aspects of each, as seen by me in the therapeutic setting and by a number of other talented psychoanalysts who have written about normal and abnormal love.

The general definition of pathological narcissism is the abnormal investment in the self (inordinate self-love) that leads to an inequality in the primary love relationship. Although the men in this study showed obvious traits of narcissistic personality disorders within their families, they also seemed to have a high capacity for functioning and success out in the world. Despite their failings, they provided for their families and offered a model of perseverance for success.

The normal self is organized around reality testing, where the adult can maintain a self-observing function and reasonable and cooperative relations with others. The normal person integrates feelings of love and hatred as a prerequisite for the capacity for normal love (Kernberg 1984).

Self-esteem is regulated by *internalized* relations with others, an integrated superego or conscience, and gratification of one's needs within the context of stable relationships and value systems. The men in this study could not fulfill these capacities effectively.

We have seen how narcissism in Kohut's view (1966) is affected when the mother's ministrations are imperfect and traumatic delays cannot be avoided. The baby tries to maintain the original wish for perfection and omnipotence by giving the adult absolute perfection and power, a reflection of his self-needs. This perfection is projected onto the parent, creating the intimate relationship between idealization and narcissism. In the transition from the practicing phase to the rapprochement crisis (when the normal child reacts to the loss of his omnipotence), the child persists in his fantasy that the world revolves around him. He protects this illusion with avoidance, denial, and devaluation, separating out perceptions of reality that don't fit with this narcissistic, grandiose self-perception.

The grandiose self is not brought into accord with reality during the rapprochement phase. The result is

> the grandiose self-representation is one of being superior, elite, exhibitionistic, with an affect of feeling perfect, special and unique. . . . While projecting this grandiose self, the person exhibits his specialness and expects perfect mirroring of his grandiosity and unique perfection. When projecting the omnipotent object [other], he idealizes the perfection of the object which he expects to share; i.e., he shares and participates in the "narcissistic glow." (Masterson 1981, 15)

As the child matures, the representation of the idealized parent changes as he is influenced by the real environment. He experiences loss due to disappointment in the parent's prohibitions and frustrations of his demands. For the healthy child, there is a normal, gradual loss of the idealized parent image and, in time, the formation of the conscience, or superego, with its standards and realistic ideals that guide the child and, later, the adult.

If the child cannot bear the frustrations and disappointments of ordinary life, he then holds on to the idealizations of childhood, according to Kohut (1966). Then the narcissistic self wants to be looked at and admired to build self-esteem.

Kernberg (1984) looks at the role of aggression in narcissistic disorders. In the extreme, the narcissist's grandiosity and self-idealization is strengthened by victory over fear and pain through the infliction of fear and pain onto others. In such cases, self-esteem is preserved by the sadistic expression of aggression (e.g., Carver with his siblings).

Mood swings are indicators of self-regard due to immature regulation of self-esteem (e.g., Carver and Wade's inflated moods when admired and accepted by others and deflated moods when they didn't feel this admiration and wish to be the center of attention).

In other narcissistic personalities, the grandiose self does not directly express aggression (e.g., neurosurgeon Clive whose aggression is seen in overactivity and diminishment of his wife's abilities). Finally, in still other cases in which there is some sublimation of aggression, the narcissist can turn it into productive behavior. A prime example from this study is Wade, who used his aggression in becoming a highly successful personal injury lawyer. This is a case where aggression has been integrated with the existing superego (to an extent).

Masterson (1981) describes how different psychoanalytic theorists view aggression in the narcissist. Kohut feels that excessive aggression is not inborn but comes from early trauma. Psychoanalysts Klein and Kernberg viewed it is an inborn trait. Masterson believes that although it may sometimes be inborn, it is more often coming from early trauma (Masterson 1981, 18).

In early development, an important function of the mother is mirroring. During this activity, the mother repeats sounds the baby makes and plays facial games where she reflects the expression on the baby's face. This activity gives the child the feeling of being "at one" with the mother. Traditionally, this stage is followed by one where the father plays a larger role, taking the child out into the "world" from ages three to six. Consequently, if this proceeds normally, the adult mature man does not experience continuous feelings of being narcissistically wounded when he cannot reach his ideals; rather, he experiences an emotion akin to longing (Kohut 1966). Ambition can then be combined with realistic goals. This occurs when a man can be motivated by his ambitions but not be driven by them or love them.

On the contrary, if the narcissistic self has been insufficiently modified because of traumatic assaults on his self-esteem during childhood, then as an adult, the man wavers between an irrational overestimation of the self and feelings of inferiority and humiliation when ambitions are upset. This has been the case for the narcissistic men in this study, whose gradual frustrations growing up were not received with adequate loving support but instead with rejection and/or overindulgence. Instead of the result being pleasurable confirmation of the "value, beauty, and loveableness of the self, there is painful shame" (Kohut 1966, 441) that the man tries to overcome with his choice of loved ones (the codependent choices).

The mother's role is complex. According to Masterson (1981), the mother may be lacking in empathy for the child's grandiose self for reasons that have to do with *her* inadequacies, rather than those of the child. The reasons may be her narcissism, her depression, or whatever mental state she is in. Furthermore, Masterson (1981) believes that from his clinical experience, the mother's ineffective mirroring may come from a specific emotional withdrawal because her specific child frustrates her own needs to shape him into a baby that maintains her own equilibrium. Masterson believes Kohut underestimates the "mother's reward for those regressive behaviors that fulfill her projections, thereby gratifying her clinging and relieving her anxiety" (1981, 23).

Regardless of the particular mother's inadequacies, which I was not privy to specifically, with each man in this study, the degree to which the man's grandiosity determined his personality depended on its integration with reality.

If the mature child's initial sense of power and greatness was not filled with traumatic disappointments, he could progress in his development. Optimally, realistic ideals and goals of the child who becomes a man are his personality's best protection against narcissistic vulnerability and shame.

Unlike guilt, shame arises when people are unable to live up to their ideals. The modification of such ideals with reality becomes the aim of narcissistic personality treatment, along with the attainment of the capacity for empathy and mature reciprocal love. A good example is Carver's recognition that he did not have to be in a club with famous people to be valuable himself.

The purpose of psychotherapy with the narcissist is to undo inordinate envy of others and idealization from whom they expect narcissistic supplies. Rio exemplified the exquisite need for perfect mirroring or idealizing, and he demonstrated profound disappointment and rage when his needs were frustrated. Each narcissist is different, but their relations with others are frequently exploitative and parasitic. Beneath the charming, engaging surface, narcissists can be cold and ruthless. They typically feel restless and bored when no new sources feed their self-regard (e.g., Clive and Wade). Because of their great need for tribute and adorations from others (e.g., Carver, Clive, Wade, and Dale's father), they are often considered to be excessively dependent. But they are, in fact, unable to depend on anyone because of a deep underlying distrust and devaluation of others and an unconscious "spoiling" of what they receive related to conflicts about unconscious envy (Kernberg 1984, 193).

Normal Love

What then is normal love? One of the main characteristics of the state of loving is when the loved one is not physically present yet feels emotionally available. This paradox consists of the ability to reproduce the image of the loved one while longing for her presence. This means the person can feel loneliness but not rejection.

The human being is also capable of taking himself as his own love in a healthy way. That is, some self-love is essential and desirable for healthy self-esteem and narcissism. Only, as noted above, when there is *neglect or excessive indulgence on the part of the caretaker*, the attachment to one's self as a love object impedes the ability to love another. (Bergmann 1987; italics added)

With maturity, the normal person can transfer love from the incestuous parental attachments to new non-incestuous adults. This is what we call "falling in love." It necessitates the ability to mourn the old love while finding the new love.

The men in this study were not fully capable of this, and thus they sought love that would aggrandize themselves, rather than true mutuality. At the same time, it is normal to

consciously or unconsciously . . . ask that the love partner be also the healer of our earlier wounds. . . . That this can be realized only on a limited scale is a source of disillusionment to many lovers . . .

The dialectics of love can be understood as a tension between these groups of wishes, the first operating in the direction of refinding, so that the new love object will be as similar as possible to the early parental images, the other opposing this process and wishing to find a person who will heal the wounds the major objects [parents] in childhood have inflicted. If a good balance between these contradictory wishes can be found, happy love becomes possible. However, at other times the conflict remains unresolved and various compromise formations take place (Bergmann 1987, 264).

Love's inability to heal all that it is charged with healing is one of the unhappy features with which every adult must come to terms. Love is especially charged with eliminating feelings of envy, jealousy, and rivalry. Indeed, the feeling that now, when one has found one's love, one need no longer envy or be jealous of anyone else is one of the most exhilarating feelings connected with love (Bergmann 1987, 265).

With treatment, the goal is the shift of narcissistic love to true reciprocal and mutual love. The narcissist has extraordinary difficulty loving because his envy and aggressive wishes can be so overwhelming. Mature love, on the other hand, occurs when idealization is changed into a more mature ability to assure a sharing of ideals when there is a clear boundary around one's self. It is important to highlight that healthy self-love goes along with and grows with love for others (Bergmann 1987).

In a love relationship, the partners enhance each other's narcissistic well-being (Bergmann 1987, 265). *Narcissism is the greatest obstacle to loving.* Those who cannot experience the tension between what they are and what they wish to be, who insist on being treated as if they already were what they imagine they are, have difficulties in loving (Bergmann 1987, 269).

According to Kohut (1971), an important result of the psychoanalysis or psychotherapy of the narcissist is the increased capacity for love of another, due to the firming up of the self-experience, which also corresponds to an increase in his professional pursuits. "The more secure a person is regarding his own acceptability, the more certain his sense of who he is, and the more safely internalized his system of values—the more self-confidently and effectively will he be able to offer his love . . . without undue fear of rejection and humiliation" (Kohut 1982, 298).

The results for the adult man are that his infantile grandiosity is gradually united with his ambitions. Then he feels a right to success. He adapts to reality with socially meaningful activities and healthy self-esteem. He also attains to a reasonable degree with "tolerance and composure" some persisting tendencies for "self-aggrandizement" and "infantile idealization," along with sociocultural attributes such as "empathy, creativity, humor, and wisdom" (Kohut 1971, 328).

Real love requires the capacity for mutuality and reciprocity in relationships. This grows with increasing maturity and experience in past and present relationships. Readers who have had such experiences are truly fortunate and live happily with their significant others. This takes continual emotional work throughout one's life.

CHAPTER TWELVE

Does Culture Affect Narcissism?

The varied constructs of culture affect how people view themselves. When we ask if culture affects narcissism, we do not mean that it is the cause of the narcissistic personality disorder but that it reinforces ideas held by people on the narcissistic spectrum. Cooper (1986) refers to the intense focus in contemporary Western civilization on private ambitions, a loss of concern with the needs of others, and a demand for immediate gratification, producing the me-first culture. We need to look at how each generation created a broad view of values held by society that affect those with NPD (or who are on the narcissistic spectrum) and how these values affect parenting practices that influence child-rearing. I will discuss each question separately, below.

The Values and Beliefs Held by Recent Generations and How They Affect Those on the Narcissistic Spectrum

Jean Twenge in *Generation Me* (2014) describes common generational cutoffs and labels: Baby Boomers, roughly 1943–60; Generation X, roughly 1961–81; and Millennials, whom she calls Generation Me, 1982–99. Her scrupulous research on nationally representative samples is based on what young people say about themselves—not what older people think of them. The trends that I will review cut across regions, racial and ethnic groups, social classes, and among men and women.

According to Twenge (2014), in the early 1960s, people would have said that the most important things were being honest, hardworking, industrious, and loyal, and caring about others. Caring about others is an issue when it comes to narcissistic views. Instead, young people in the GenMe generation are taught to put their own needs first and focus on feeling good about themselves, rather than to follow social rules or favor group over individual needs.

For his book *Souls in Transition and Lost in Transition* (2009), Christian Smith interviewed eighteen- to twenty-three-year-olds. He found that most young Americans espouse moral individualism, which means that morality (what each person thinks is right or wrong) is a personal choice. Those interviewed made statements such as "People don't have a duty to help others, but it's up to each individual." Smith concluded that most emerging adults seem unaware of any particular sources of moral reasoning and decide for themselves what is and isn't moral and immoral. There is increased tolerance, but with the proviso that everyone is free to decide for himself which rules to abide by. Helping others is rarely one of these rules. This societal shift certainly has a bearing on narcissistic attitudes that dismiss or don't understand empathy—that is, being in another's shoes.

Moral views were further elaborated in a 2012 study of high school students reported by Twenge (2014). Twenge found that 57 percent of students agreed that in the real world, successful people did whatever they had to do to win, even if others considered it cheating. The majority believed that "the ends justified the means." This reminds me of Rio, who believed that manipulation and exploitation were just the way things are. It also makes me reflect on Clive, who did his kids' homework and didn't consider it cheating if it improved their scores (which it didn't in the long run). And it makes me think of Carver at the beginning of his treatment, who had his own view of what made people successful: he believed that networking with the rich and famous (rather than taking on hard-working jobs to prepare for industrious careers) was the best path. For each of these examples, it was a succeed-at-all-costs mentality. This breakdown of the means to reach what one defines as success reaches all the way to the top, including vast business scandals such as those at WorldCom and Enron and the mortgage meltdown of the late 2000s. This demonstrates, according to Twenge (2014), that breaking rules and telling lies in an attempt to make more money is "just fine." This is the ruthlessness of narcissism.

Entitlement is another issue of narcissists. GenMe'ers believe that they do not have to recognize authority but are entitled to do just as they please. Carver at first would often abide by this standard.

Technology today plays an important role in disregarding others' feelings. Smartphones with frequent texting result in blunt, short phrases where you don't see the receiver's reactions and are blind to empathic comments. Additionally, Facebook and other social networks make it is easy to attack people and get away with it. Twenge (2014) says, "Technology has in some ways made us meaner—or at least given us an anonymous venue for being so" (53).

Twenge (2014) also discusses the term "self-esteem," which was very prevalent by the 1990s: self-love was paramount. A multitude of Americans felt that life should be focused on the needs of the self. Historically, this self-focus began with the Boomers and then increased exponentially by the time the GenMe folks were born. Twenge (2014) reports that "Since they were small children, GenMe'ers were taught to put themselves first" (63). Surely, this attitude reinforces narcissism. By 2013, the *Oxford English Dictionary*'s word of the year was *selfie*—sharing pictures of oneself with the world—and by January 2014, people were competing to put their favorite picture of themselves in the Selfie Olympics.

Schools focused on designing programs to promote self-esteem. For example, Twenge (2014) notes a program called *Self-Science: The Subject Is Me*. Schools mentioned self-esteem in their mission statements—even as the emphasis on testing in the 1990s grew. Children were taught that it was not only acceptable but desirable to be preoccupied with oneself and to praise oneself. Furthermore, grade inflation was on the rise, without clarifying the skills needed to get those grades. Kids became accustomed from elementary school through college to always getting higher grades than they may have actually earned, as if they deserved these grades. The idea was that we need to make our kids feel good about themselves in general, without specifying why.

The problem with the emphasis on self-esteem is that it was putting the cart before the horse. Self-esteem didn't lead to accomplishment; hard work, achievement, and caring for others led to high self-esteem. In her book *The Smartest Kids in the World* (2014), Amanda Ripley echoes that notion when she describes the most successful kids internationally as those with vigor, persistence, toleration of frustration, and self-discipline. Narcissistic self-love and empty self-esteem do not lead to happiness or achievement. Talent and hard work—not an inflated self-belief system—lead to feelings of success.

The GenMe era grew, along with technology and social networking. Narcissism was promoted by the focus on numbers of followers on Twitter and Facebook. Twenge (2014) cites a study that found that "narcissists, especially those high in feelings of superiority or exhibitionism, posted to Twitter and Facebook more often" than others (104). It seems these sites generally promote social connectedness without the depth of actual relationships that foster deep involvement with others or offer help to others. This is not to say that blogging and connections made on the internet were not later developed into realistic relations with others, but that this was not the norm.

Values and beliefs in our culture that affect narcissistic men are often gender-biased, teaching us that to be masculine is to be narcissistic and violent. This is a topic worth investigating by itself; however, it needs to be mentioned because the narcissist diminishes the woman who is dominated by him. I'm not suggesting that narcissism and violent behavior are synonymous, but the belief system of the narcissistic man may have been affected by other men in his life who have taught him that men are superior to women. When Wade and his father were so disconnected from Wade's mother's brutality (hair-pulling, hitting, overt critical attitudes) toward her daughters, male domination was reinforced. When Clive comments, "Maybe the women who were hurt by men in the #MeToo movement did something to encourage it," Laura knew he was a misogynist—even if he denied it. Such biased beliefs that men should be dominant in intimate relationships need to be addressed actively in our society; such men need to learn views alternative to their upbringing. Society's emphasis shouldn't just be on what makes the woman vulnerable to the narcissistic man but also on what makes the narcissistic man believe he has a right to dominate and intimidate girls and women. Many female victims of domestic violence, as reported by journalist and professor Rachel Louise Snyder, say that they dated narcissistic men (Snyder 2019, 119). Snyder said, "I came to learn that there is a high incidence of narcissism in [violent] perpetrators" who suffer from "toxic masculinity" (10). While I don't make correlations or links between narcissism and violence in men, Snyder takes up the challenge of supporting men with programs that treat those who "know intimately the struggle of being surrounded by violence and trying to break free from the behavior" (133).

Snyder also noted that "the clinical narcissism of these men kept them from being able to really see how their behavior impacted their victims" (133). David Adams, developer of the first batterer intervention program—Emerge, a program for controlling and abusive behavior—is quoted by Snyder in her report:

> "Narcissism filters how they see everything." . . . Extreme narcissism is at the root of understanding batterers, and while we may think of narcissists as conspicuous misfits who can't

stop talking about themselves, in fact they are often high-functioning, charismatic, and professionally successful. The narcissists are "hiding among us . . . and they're clustered at the top." . . . Such people are not easy to identify, in part because they have outsized people skills, and "we live in a world that is increasingly narcissistic. We extol success more than we extol anything." (156)

Snyder continues to include Adams's quote in her report by stating that Adams points to

the kind of "charismatic narcissist who is worshiped by others." This is the kind of white-collar batterer who—through money and connections—manages to evade judicial and law enforcement systems. A man for whom status and reputation are everything. . . . They are impossible to divine from the general population. (156) . . .

If you have this outsized view of yourself, and you suffer narcissistic injury, you'll lash out . . . [Such narcissists] "live and die by their image." When that image is compromised, say they're discovered lying or a secret they've borne is discovered [like unemployment or bankruptcy,] they lash out and "impose" their solution on their partners and children. The solution in extreme cases is homicide. (164) . . .

[On the contrary, it is also reported] how emotional abuse [is viewed as] being so much worse than physical abuse . . . [Snyder says one] domestic violence advocate told me, "[Narcissists] are so charming, and the victim comes off as very negative." His narcissism, in other words, didn't even allow the room for her to care for herself. (157, 158)

Le Droit du Seigneur (The Right of the Lord)

We can ask, "What is the basis for the role of narcissism in our society?" and "Is there an evolutionary role of narcissism?" These questions are raised by Carl Sagan and Ann Druyan in *Shadows of Forgotten Ancestors* (1992) when they inadvertently look at the basis in evolution for narcissism by studying animals' behaviors. They speculate,

> Now suppose you grow up in a society in which such behavior [dominant males preferring copulation with attractive females] is the community standard. . . . Would it be surprising if this powerful symbol of dominance and submission were generalized in the gestural and postural vocabulary of the status-obsessed males? (213)

Speaking of a broad range of animals, they comment that the female "could smell dominance" and that "there is literally a chemistry between them, the odor of power." One time heavy-weight boxing champion Mike Tyson explained his scattershot propositioning of virtually every contestant at a beauty pageant with "Dominant males give off effluvium, the same pheromone that celebrities do." Former US Secretary of State Kissinger, not known for his looks, explained a beautiful actress's attraction to him in these words: "Power is the greatest aphrodisiac." Dominance and testosterone seem to be of central importance in understanding human behavior and social systems (212, 238).

Thus, there appears to be evolution at play; narcissism in our society and political structure today traces back to our primal ancestors.

> Calm and assured, the alpha male does not scowl at his nearly prostrate subordinate. . . . Generally, he approaches with a swagger, arms akimbo. It's hard not to see here the rudiments of government administration of justice. . . . Regal touching . . . in a sea of outstretched hands seems familiar enough to us—reminiscent, say, of the President striding down the central aisle of the House of Representatives just before the State of the Union address, especially when he's riding high in the polls. The future King Edward VIII on his world tour, Senator Robert Kennedy in his presidential campaign, and countless other political leaders have returned home black and blue from the grasp of their enthusiastic followers. (296)

This is part of our current culture that Snyder bravely addresses today—just as Sanger and Druyan speculated in 1992. If narcissism is this engrained into our society, parents need to be ever more present and aware of how their actions can play a part in their child's future narcissistic attitudes.

Parenting Practices that Emphasize Self-Love

It is healthy for parents to care about the self-esteem of their children, but what is striking is the increase in the momentum of self-esteem as a *primary* focus in the family. It is also interesting that parents often tell their kids they are special without indicating why. So, kids get an overblown sense of themselves without understanding their specific merits. They don't end up learning what to do or think and feel in order to raise their self-esteem on their own. Parenting books and magazines emphasize building self-esteem. Again, what is striking isn't this good feature of healthy parenting; it is that the emphasis wasn't based on achievement and care for others, leading to high self-esteem.

Self-esteem seems to be a concept constructed by parents when, in fact, what is pertinent and important is their child's self-regulation of their self-esteem. Self-esteem is the difference between the child's ideals for himself and what is realistic for himself. If the ideals are too high compared to what is realistic, then low self-esteem results; the ideals are only meant to guide. This is in line with psychoanalyst Jacobson's (1954) formulation that self-esteem is "expressive of the discrepancy or harmony between the self-representations and the wishful concepts of the self" (123). When parents just tell their children that they are winners without specifying why, the child does not learn how to regulate his self-esteem on his own. Children are left helpless in being able to integrate their actual self in the moment with their experience of the ideal shape of the self as a winner. The child begins to view himself, instead, only as a winner *or* loser, with no gradations of understanding of the multifaceted quality of his self-esteem. If he views himself as a hopeless loser, he may develop a depressive reaction. Depression is present in the wide realm of narcissistic disorders; it reflects one's attitude toward the self that can be ambivalently loved and hated.

According to Cooper (1986), narcissism has often been used as a synonym for self-esteem or as a broad reference to a concentration of psychological interest upon the self. Parents who focus on self-esteem may not realize the depths of this emphasis and attention. Developmental needs and cultural forces are involved. Narcissistic rage could be prevented by simply acknowledging the limitations of oneself as a separate, imperfect being in a world of imperfect people. Parents may be trying to cope with this existential phenomenon themselves, and they may feel helpless in a complex society.

As early as 1939, Horney describes the loss of the "real me" as occurring under different parental conditions, such as parental pressure and intimidation, when the child suffers impairment of self-sufficiency, self-reliance, and initiative. Self-inflation or narcissism is an attempt to cope with these tendencies.

Then there are children raised in the GenMe era, where there was a shift from the benevolent authority-centered family. These children, who were too often raised with too much overindulgence, were misled into believing they should have and be able to do whatever they want or dream of doing—as if wishing would make it so. Some adults made things seem easier than they were so that their kids grew up with unrealistic expectations, overconfidence, and ultimately, the inability to tolerate failure and learn from mistakes. Children were often permitted to make their own choices when young, even if they weren't developmentally old enough to make those decisions, leaving them exhausted and not the possessors of high self-esteem.

Following are two examples of types of parenting that can lead to a narcissistic child. In the first case, the parent is overinvested in the child and indulges the child endlessly. There is a true lack of boundaries. The second case describes the parent who has interrupted or intermittent interest and attention to their child, thus causing their child to fear that when they are out of sight of the parent, they are out of mind of the parent. For the parent in this second example, the need for self-gratification is realized when the child is treated as if nonexistent. There is a withdrawal of the demands of parenting (Furman and Furman 1998). Both overinvestment and intermittent investment can result in narcissism in children. The narcissistic distribution varies in each case between parent and child. A reasonable amount of contact would rather be understood by parents who know their specific child's needs well, so they can provide what the child learns to expect as a routine amount of contact to regularly rely upon.

Thus, the ability of parents to maintain a constantly available narcissistic investment in their children varies widely on a spectrum. On the one end are parents overanxiously preoccupied with their children, common to the GenMe era; theirs is an unhealthy investment that is deleterious to the child's development. At the other end of the spectrum are parents unable to enter the developmental phase of parenthood by investing in their children, causing extreme deprivation. These are people who became parents and regret losing their lifestyle of the self-centered GenMe'er. Between these extremes are unusual variations, such as the abovementioned parent with intermittent investment in the child (who is never secure in the availability of the parent). Being treated temporarily as nonexistent to the parent creates a major narcissistic injury. This may or may not be related to the parent's aggression. If this treatment is conscious to the parent, we can ascribe aggression to their lack of response. But if it is unconscious, then there is a certain lack of maturity not necessarily related to aggression toward the child. In either case, the child reacts with low self-esteem ("I am nothing"), which may be warded off by narcissistic overestimation of the self or narcissistic rage at the disinterested parent. These may be parents who have very low self-esteem themselves and who focus on replenishing their *own* narcissistic needs when they are disconnected from their children. The children and the parents (who were also decathected or disconnected emotionally from their parents as children) need to straighten out how their ability to love themselves can be worked out by understanding how they were loved. Furman and Furman (1998) put this clearly when they state,

We invest in others, in things outside ourselves, as we invest in ourselves and we invest in ourselves as our parents initially invested in us. It may be that it is the nature of those investments that ultimately determines the mature harmonious function of the personality. (45)

How do marriages fare with and without children? Although economics may play a part, Twenge (2014) notes that the younger generations experience a 42 percent greater drop in marital satisfaction after having children than do previous generations. This seems likely due to the radical shift away from the self that parenthood requires. I question this data because it isn't clear if the marital satisfaction comes after decades of raising kids or just after the initial impact that babies have on family life, which is exhausting and focused on the infant. In fact, now that parenting is more of a choice than a duty, it would seem that there are more older parents who have had their career successes and carefully and most wishfully want to have families with children.

Parents today seem to put more pressure on adolescents to compete vigorously for the best college acceptances they can attain, while also ironically blaming teachers too often for their supposedly special kids' low grades based on insufficient hard work.

GenMe teens feel a great deal of pressure from parents and their schools to get into a prestigious college and be successful, which includes being famous and very well-off. This may account for high burnout among college-age kids, who have spent their high school years highly motivated and competitive to be better than their peers academically and in athletics—only to find that acceptance rates of even stellar achievers are often low. Parents are pushing their kids much harder than before, and kids are paying for it in depression, anxiety, and high levels of stress. If self-love is primary, this pressure certainly bumps down their self-esteem. Plus, the facts are in that things are harder in the college and work world for the GenMe generation. Their young expectations are turning into deep disillusionments; they face difficulty getting jobs and residencies that will allow them their early high expectations of being rich and famous. These expectations lead to feelings of a loss of control over their futures. As they face reality, they feel misled by their parents' expectations of their specialness and their focus on themselves. Loneliness and depression often result.

Let me conclude this study with the words of Martin Bergmann once again: "Narcissism is the greatest obstacle to loving. Those who cannot experience the tension between what they are and what they wish to be, who insist on being treated as if they already were what they imagine they are, have difficulties in loving" (1987, 269).

These cogent words of wisdom exemplify individuals' needs to recognize if narcissistic people are in their lives; how to cope with them, so as not to detract from one's own happiness; and how to pursue loving and successful relationships through the generations. In this complex study, it is exceptionally important to respect the need for compassion for the narcissistic men who have suffered as children in their formative years, for the women living with them and raising children with them, and for the youngsters being parented by them. As we have seen, there is significant hope for those in these circumstances provided by learning about the multifaceted aspects of considerable psychotherapeutic treatment and about the multiple, often contradictory, characteristics of pathological narcissism. This knowledge helps those in our society in general become better informed and capable of understanding this intriguing, significant disorder that is often hidden from view by misleading outer appearances of success and accomplishment, as well as the invisible lack of well-being in the lives of some families.

REFERENCES

Ablon, S. 2018. *Changeable: How Collaborative Problem Solving Changes Lives at Home, at School, and at Work*. New York: Penguin Random House.

Alexander, T. 2003. "Narcissism and the Experience of Crying. Brit." *J. Psychother.* 20(1):27–38.

American Psychiatric Association. 2014. *Diagnostic and Statistical Manual of Mental Disorders*, 5th ed. Arlington, VA: American Psychiatric Association.

Arabi, S. 2017. *Power: Surviving and Thriving after Narcissistic Abuse*. Brooklyn, NY: Thought Catalog Books.

Bailey-Rug, C. 2015. *Children and Narcissistic Personality Disorder: A Guide for Parents*. Middletown, DE: Lulu.

Baker, D. L. 1986. *Narcissus and the Lover: Mythic Recovery and Reinvention in Sceve's Delie*. Stanford University: Anma Libri.

Baker M., and H. S. Baker. 1987. "Heinz Kohut's Self-Psychology: An Overview." *Am J Psychiatry*. 144(1):1–9.

Barr, C. T., P. K. Kerig, K. K. Stellwagen, and T. D. Barry, eds. 2011. *Narcissism and Machiavellianism in Youth: Implications for the Development of Adaptive and Maladaptive Behavior*. Washington, DC: American Psychological Association.

Bergmann, M. 1987. *The Anatomy of Loving: The Story of Man's Quest to Know What Love Is*. New York: Columbia University Press.

Blanck, G., and R. Blanck. 1974. *Ego Psychology: Theory and Practice*. New York: Columbia University Press.

Bleiberg, E. 1994. "Normal and pathological narcissism in adolescence." *Am. J. Psychother.* 48(1):30–51.

Brown, N. W. 2008. *Children of the Self-Absorbed: A Grown-Up's Guide to Getting Over a Narcissistic Parent*. Oakland, CA: New Harbinger Publications, Inc.

Choi, J., B. Jeong, M. L. Rohan, A. M. Polcari, and M. H. Teicher. 2009. "Preliminary Evidence for White Matter Tract Abnormalities in Young Adults Exposed to Parental Verbal Abuse." *Biological Psychiatry* 65(3):227–234.

Cooper, A. M. 1986. "Narcissism." In *Essential Papers on Narcissism*. New York and London: New York University Press.

Deutsch, H. 1987. *Selected Problems of Adolescence with Special Emphasis on Group Formation*. New York: International Universities Press, Inc. pp. 1–135.

Erikson, Erik H. 1950. *Childhood and Society*. New York: Norton.

Fjelstad, M. n.d. "14 Signs You're Dealing with a Narcissist." MindBodyGreen.com. Accessed October 6, 2019. https://www.mindbodygreen.com/articles/14-signs-of-narcissism.

Freud, S. 1914. "On Narcissism: An Introduction." *The Standard Edition of the Complete Psychological Works of Sigmund Freud*, vol. XIV. pp. 73–104.

Freud, S. 1920. "Inhibitions, Symptoms and Anxiety." *The Standard Edition of the Psychological Works of Sigmund Freud*, vol. XX. pp. 87–156.

Furman, R., and E. Furman. 1998. "Intermittent Decathexis—A Type of Parental Dysfunction." In *Narcissistic Disorders in Children and Adolescents: Diagnosis and Treatment*, P. Beren, ed. Northvale, New Jersey, London: Jason Aronson, Inc.

Grant, D., and E. Harrari. 2011. "Empathy in Psychoanalytic Theory and Practice." *Psychoanl. Inquiry* (14):3–16.

HealthPrep.com. 2016. "Signs of a Narcissist to Look Out For." Accessed October 6, 2019. https://healthprep.com/mental-health/narcissist-signs/.

Hollman, L. 2015. *Unlocking Parental Intelligence: Finding Meaning in Your Child's Behavior*. Sanger, CA: Familius.

Horney, K. 1939. *New Ways in Psychoanalysis*. New York: Norton.

Jacobson, E. 1954. "The Self and the Object World: Vicissitudes of Their Infantile Cathexes and Their Influence on Ideational Affective Development." *Psychoanalytic Study of the Child* 9:75–127. New York: International Universities Press.

Johnson, B. D., and L. Berdahl. January 29, 2017. "Childhood Roots of Narcissistic Personality Disorder." PsychologyToday.com. Accessed October 6, 2019. https://www.psychologytoday.com/us/blog/warning-signs-parents/201701/childhood-roots-narcissistic-personality-disorder/.

Kernberg, O. 1984. *Severe Personality Disorders: Psychotherapeutic Strategies*. New Haven and London: Yale University Press.

Kernberg, P. F., A. Weiner, and K. Bardenstein. 2000. *Personality Disorders in Children and Adolescents*. New York: Basic Books.

Kitron, D. 2011. "Empathy: The Indispensable Ingredient in the Impossible Profession." *Psychoanal. Inquiry* 31(1):17.

Kohut, H. 1966. "Forms and Transformations of Narcissism." *J of the Amer. Psychological Assn.* 14:243–272.

Kohut, H. 1968. "The Psychoanalytic Treatment of Narcissistic Disorders—Outline of a Systematic Approach." *Psychoanal. St. Child* 23(8):86–87.

Kohut, H. 1971. *The Analysis of the Self: A Systematic Approach to the Psychoanalytic Treatment of Narcissistic Personality Disorders*. New York: International Universities Press.

Loewald, H. W. 1960. "On the Therapeutic Action of Psychoanalysis." *International Journal of Psycho-Analysis* 41:16–33.

Mahler, M., F. Pine, and A. Bergman. 1975. *The Psychological Birth of the Infant*. New York: Basic Books.

Martin, J. A. M. 1964. "Disorders of Human Communication 4." In *Voice, Speech and Language in the Child: Development and Disorder*. New York: Springer-Verlag.

Masterson, J. 1981. *The Narcissistic and Borderline Disorders: An Integrated Developmental Approach*. New York: Brunner/Mazel, Publishers.

Muslin, H. 1985. *Heinz Kohut: Beyond the Pleasure Principle, Contributions to Psychoanalysis*. In *Beyond Freud: A Study of Modern Psychoanalytic Theorists*, Reppen, J., ed. Hillsdale, NJ: Lawrence Erlbaum Associates, Inc. pp. 203–229.

Ornstein, P. H., and J. Kay. 1990. "Development of Psychoanalytic Self Psychology: a Historical-Conceptual Overview." In *Review of Psychiatry*, Tasman A., S. M. Goldfinger, and C. A. Kaufmann, eds. American Psychiatric Press, Inc. pp. 303–22.

Payson, E. D. 2017. *Discovering the Healthy Self: and Meaningful Resistance to Toxic Narcissism*. Royal Oak, MI: Julian Day Publications.

Pine, F. 1994. "The Era of Separation-Individuation." *Psychoanal. Inquiry* 14(1):4–24.

Pressman, R., and S. Donaldson-Pressman. 1994. *The Narcissistic Family*. San Francisco, CA: Jossey-Bass.

Psychology Today. n.d. "Narcissism." Accessed October 6, 2019. https://www.psychologytoday.com/us/basics/narcissism.

Ripley, A. 2014. *The Smartest Kids in the World and How They Got That Way*. New York: Simon and Schuster.

Rosenberg, R. 2013. *The Human Magnet Syndrome: Why We Love People Who Hurt Us*. Claire, WI: Pesi Publications.

Rothstein, A. 1986. "The Theory of Narcissism: An Object-Relations Perspective." In *Essential Papers on Narcissism*, Morrison, A. P., ed. New York: New York University.

Sagan, C., and A. Druyan. 1992. *Shadows of Forgotten Ancestors*. New York: Ballantine Books.

Shakespeare, W. 1996. *Updated Edition Folger Shakespeare Library: Richard III.* Edited by B. A. Mowat and P. Werstine. New York: Simon and Schuster.

Siskind, D. 1994. "Max and His Diaper: An Example of the Interplay of Arrests in Psychosexual Development and the Separation-Individuation Process." *Psychoanal. Inq.* 14(1):58–82.

Smith, C. 2009. *Souls in Transition and Lost in Transition.* New York: Oxford University Press.

Snyder, R. L. 2019. *No Visible Bruises: What We Don't Know about Domestic Violence Can Kill Us.* New York: Bloomsbury Publishing.

Stern, D. 1985. *The Interpersonal World of the Infant: A View from Psychoanalysis and Developmental Psychology.* New York: Basic Books.

Teicher, M. 2006. "Sticks, Stones, and Hurtful Words: Relative Effects of Various Forms of Childhood Maltreatment." *American Journal of Psychiatry* 163(6):993.

Twenge, J. 2014. *Generation Me: Why Today's Young Americans Are More Confident, Assertive, Entitled—and More Miserable than Ever Before.* New York: Atria.

Twenge, J. 2017. *iGen: Why Today's Super-Connected Kids Are Growing Up Less Rebellious, More Tolerant, Less Happy—and Completely Unprepared for Adulthood and What That Means for the Rest of Us.* New York: Simon and Schuster.

Websdale, N. 2010. *Familicidal Hearts: The Emotional Styles of 211 Killers.* New York: Oxford University Press.

White, M. T. 1986. "Self Relations, Object Relations, and Pathological Narcissism." In *Essential Papers on Narcissism*, Morrison, A., ed. New York: New York University.

INDEX

SYMBOLS

E

F

G

About the Author

LAURIE HOLLMAN, PHD, is a psychoanalyst with specialized clinical training in infant-parent, child, adolescent, and adult psychotherapy. She specializes in modern parent-child relationships and is an award-winning, three-time author. She has been on the faculties of New York University and the Society for Psychoanalytic Training and Research, among others. She has written extensively on parenting for various publications, including the *Psychoanalytic Study of the Child*, *The International Journal of Infant Observation*, *The Inner World of the Mother*, *Newsday's Parents & Children Magazine*, and *Long Island Parent* in New York. She blogged for *Huffington Post* and currently blogs for *Thrive Global*. She also writes for *Active Family Magazine* in San Francisco and is a parenting expert for *Good Housekeeping* and *Bustle Lifestyle*. Her Mom's Choice Award–winning books are: *Unlocking Parental Intelligence: Finding Meaning in Your Child's Behavior*; *The Busy Parent's Guide to Managing Anxiety in Children and Teens: The Parental Intelligence Way*; and *The Busy Parent's Guide to Managing Anger in Children and Teens: The Parental Intelligence Way*. She has also recently written *The Busy Parent's Guide to Managing Technology with Children and Teens* and *The Busy Parent's Guide to Managing Exhaustion: The Parental Intelligence Way*. Learn more on lauriehollmanphd.com.

Dr. Hollman is married, with two spirited, loving adult sons.

About Familius

Visit Our Website: www.familius.com

Familius is a global trade publishing company that publishes books and other content to help families be happy. We believe that the family is the fundamental unit of society and that happy families are the foundation of a happy life. We recognize that every family looks different, and we passionately believe in helping all families find greater joy. To that end, we publish books for children and adults that invite families to live the Familius Nine Habits of Happy Family Life: *love together, play together, learn together, work together, talk together, heal together, read together, eat together,* and *laugh together.* Founded in 2012, Familius is located in Sanger, California.

Connect

- Facebook: www.facebook.com/paterfamilius
- Twitter: @familiustalk, @paterfamilius1
- Pinterest: www.pinterest.com/familius
- Instagram: @familiustalk

> **THE MOST IMPORTANT WORK YOU EVER DO WILL BE WITHIN THE WALLS OF YOUR OWN HOME.**

CPSIA information can be obtained
at www.ICGtesting.com
Printed in the USA
FSHW010734151119
64113FS

9 781641 70233